The dramatic rock temple of Tanah Lot ("Land in the Sea") in Tabanan, on the west coast of Bali, is one of the island's most dramatic and most sacred sights, dedicated to the God of the Sea, Dewa Baruna. Said to have been founded in the middle of the 16th century by the Javanese temple builder, Nirartha, it is now visited by millions and is the site of regular festivals and celebrations.

FACING PAGE A small rice storage barn in a modern compound.

BALINESE ARCHITECTURE

A GUIDE TO TRADITIONAL AND MODERN DESIGN

Text by **Julian Davison**
Illustrations by **Bruce Granquist,**
Mubinas Hanafi and **Nengah Enu**

TUTTLE Publishing
Tokyo | Rutland, Vermont | Singapore

Contents

Balinese Architecture and Belief Systems

The archetypal Balinese residence—from the humblest abode to the grandest palace—reflects an ancient architectural tradition which has its origins, at least in part, in India. Metaphysics, Hindu religious beliefs, cosmology, ritual, function and climate all combine to determine the location, shape and function of buildings.

Most often, the Balinese residence comprises a collection of low-profile pavilions set in a walled compound (*pekarangan*), surrounded by fruit trees and ornamental shrubs. Each building is placed on a low plinth and surmounted by a hipped roof clad with clay pantiles or grass thatch. Some structures are open-sided, while others are enclosed by masonry walls. Each building has a specific function.

Microcosm and Macrocosm

Balinese architecture is grounded in a metaphysics that presents the universe as an integrated whole, where each part participates in the existence of every other part, and where the microcosm is perceived as a reflection of the macrocosm.

Correct orientation in space, combined with ideas of ritual purity and pollution, are key concepts, providing a cosmological framework for maintaining a harmony between man and the rest of the universe. This view of the world derives from the Hindu idea of a divine cosmic order (dharma).

Balinese Hinduism

Indian religious beliefs in Southeast Asia date from the time of Christ when Indian merchants first developed trade links with the region. Balinese Hinduism, however, probably owes more to Javanese influences between the 14th and 16th centuries than it does directly to the Indian subcontinent. This was the era of the mighty East Javanese Majapahit empire (1292–c. 1525) whose political and cultural influence at its height extended over much of the Indonesian archipelago, including Bali. The Majapahit dynasty was the last in a long line of Hindu-Buddhist kingdoms in Java which in earlier centuries had been responsible for building the great temple complexes at Borobudur and Prambanan.

Divided into Three

The tripartite division of the universe dovetails with the concept of *tri angga*, which assumes that everything in the natural world can be divided into three parts. *Utama*, which denotes things that are "high" or "above," is identified with mountains and, by extension, the gods who dwell there, heaven and the ancestors, and all that is pure or sacred. *Nista* denotes things that are "low" or "below," including the sea and any malevolent spirits, hell and the dead, the impure and the profane. Man occupies the middle ground of *madya*, the mundane world of everyday existence, a hinterland that stretches from the seashore to the foothills of the central mountain range. The human body can be similarly divided into three parts—head, torso, and feet. This tripartite scheme of things extends to the components of the simplest built structure—the base, the walls or posts, and the roof.

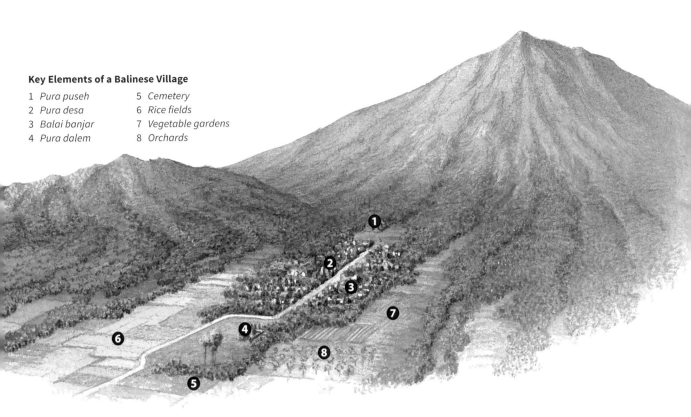

Key Elements of a Balinese Village

1 *Pura puseh*
2 *Pura desa*
3 *Balai banjar*
4 *Pura dalem*
5 *Cemetery*
6 *Rice fields*
7 *Vegetable gardens*
8 *Orchards*

By the end of the 15th century, however, the power of Majapahit had waned as new Muslim polities were establishing themselves along the north coast of Java and elsewhere in the archipelago.

The final collapse came in the early years of the 16th century, and led to the removal of the royal court to Bali, where earlier generations of Majapahit colonizers had established themselves as the local elite. These refugees included artisans, scholars, priests, and aristocrats, and they brought with them the religion, manners, and artistic conventions of the Javanese court. Over time, these cultural orientations became assimilated as part of the island's unique cultural tradition, giving rise to a singularly Balinese style of Hinduism suffused with Buddhist influences and indigenous animism.

A Tripartite Universe

Balinese architecture is based on a set of cosmological orientations and ritual considerations which influence most aspects of life. The Balinese universe comes in multiples of three. The most basic is the division of the cosmos into three domains: the underworld (*buhr*), the realm of evil and malevolent spirits; the world of human beings (*bhuwa*h); and the heavens above (*swah*), occupied by the gods and deified ancestors.

ABOVE **Balinese villages are usually arranged on a linear axis between the sea and the mountains. The temple of origin (*pura puseh*)—dedicated to the community's founders—is at the uphill (*kaja*) end of the village, as befits deified ancestors, while the temple of the dead (*pura dalem*) and the cemetery are at the downhill or seaward (*kelod*) end, reflecting the polluting nature of death.**

BELOW **Pura Ulun Danu Bratan ("Temple at the Source of Lake Bratan") is one of Bali's holiest sites—lying inside the massive Mt. Batur caldera in central Bali, on the northern shores of a huge crater lake. The temple consists of four compounds, two of which are on tiny islets in the lake and contain pagoda-like structures called *meru* representing the holy mountain of Hindu cosmology—a resting place for the gods. This deep crater lake serves as a massive water reservoir for Bali, feeding springs scattered along the flanks of the volcano. Over many centuries, the Balinese have created elaborate networks of irrigation channels and rice terraces fed by these springs. Periodically they give thanks to the gods of the lake who provide this live-giving water.**

The Nawa-sanga Compass Points

The Balinese compass (*nawa-sanga*) includes the four cardinal directions, their intermediaries, and a central area. Each point is linked to a particular deity—Hindu in origin—and has symbolic and ritual associations, such as corresponding numbers, colors, magical syllables, and mystical attributes. The compass provides a comprehensive framework for the orientation of buildings on Bali.

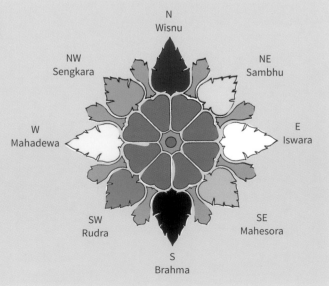

N
Wisnu

NW
Sengkara

NE
Sambhu

W
Mahadewa

E
Iswara

SW
Rudra

SE
Mahesora

S
Brahma

FAR LEFT, TOP **Rice terraces outside of Ubud.**

FAR LEFT, BOTTOM **Villagers receive a blessing of holy water during the Kuningan New Year's celebration.**

LEFT **Bali's dramatic topography has shaped the Balinese concepts of cosmology and architecture. The island's central volcanoes are all considered sacred; the highest peak, Mt. Agung, seen here in the background, is the highest and most sacred of all. Rivers and roads run north-south down from the peaks to the ocean. Most villages and houses are oriented along this north-south axis.**

This model can be mapped on to the local topography where natural divisions occur between the mountains at the center of the island, the hinterland, and the sea. The mountains are the holiest part of the island—the main places of worship are there—while the sea is cast as impure, home to malevolent spirits and evil influences. The coastal plains and foothills, the intermediate realm, is the proper abode of man.

A Sense of Place

For the Balinese, everything has its correct place in the world, with the gods being placed on high, the malevolent spirits being positioned in the lowest regions, and mankind sandwiched between the two. Proper positioning in relation to the rest of the world is important for maintaining harmonious relations with the rest of the universe. Thus, Balinese architecture is mediated not only by measurement but by various spatial orientations. These ensure that buildings and their occupants are favorably placed.

The two principal directions in Balinese cosmology and the most important points of reference are called *kaja* and *kelod*. *Kaja* is defined as "upstream" or "toward the mountains," the central mountain range in Bali being identified as the abode of the gods. *Kelod*, conversely, lies the opposite way, "downstream" or "toward the sea," considered a region of great impurity and malign influences, and the home of monstrous demons and malevolent spirits. In southern Bali, where most of the population live, *kaja* and *kelod* roughly correspond to north and south respectively, but on the opposite side of the island the reverse is, of course, the case. *Kangin* (east), *kauh* (west) and the intermediary compass points are almost of equal importance.

Building a House in Bali

Building a Balinese house is as much a ritual process as it is a practical undertaking. Correct alignment with the sacred mountain, Gunung Agung, is an important consideration but many other ritual prescriptions govern the orientation, building methods, and dimensions of every kind of built structure in the Balinese architectural lexicon.

The rules relating to the ritual and practical aspects of Balinese architecture are codified in sacred texts deposited with the village priests. These ancient documents, inscribed by hand on lontar palm manuscripts, are called the *Asta Kosali* or *Asta Kosalia*. This title probably derives from the Sanskrit words *hasta* (hand) and *kausalya* (skill).

The *Asta Kosali* is consulted and interpreted in relation to specific circumstances by the *undagi*, or local architect-builder, who is an expert in rituals relating to architecture. Every aspect of construction and design, including shape, size, directional orientation, and position of buildings in relation to other structures, is exhaustively documented in this Balinese building manual, which even prescribes the type of social background from which the builders of a particular type of structure should be recruited.

These texts are usually written in what is known as Jawa Kuno or Kawi, a semi-sacred language used in prayers and invocations to the gods. Kawi is never used in daily life and, though related to Balinese, is virtually unintelligible to anyone who has not received a formal education in it. Although these building regulations are available for inspection by anyone who wishes to consult them, the arcane nature of the language means that, in practice, only language experts and priests are likely to do so. Instead, carpenters and builders generally learn their trade by a kind of informal apprenticeship and the sacred texts are usually referred to only when there is disagreement about procedures or when constructing rarely erected types of building.

Building for the Future

The design and construction of a Balinese dwelling is literally seen as determining the fate of its future occupants and the *Asta Kosali* provides a detailed account of the unfortunate consequences that will result from disregarding the rules. Failure to adhere

Changing Units of Measurement

Balinese units of measurement change their values depending on how many are used in a particular situation and their symbolic significance. The unit *tampak hatis*, which is the length of the house owner's foot and is used to measure the distance between the various structures in the compound, has eight distinct significances, after which the cycle repeats itself. Rather like "Tinker, tailor, soldier, sailor"—the children's game of counting cherry stones—the final unit in the overall measurement will determine the character of the dimension and hence the qualities of the building to which it relates, sealing the fate of its occupants, as it were. A little extra is always added to the overall dimension—in the case of *tampak hatis*, the width of the house owner's foot—which is said to bring "life" (*urip*) to the building.

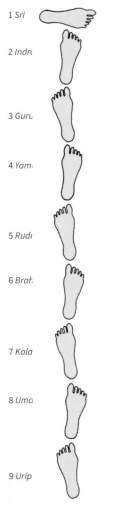

1 *Sri*

2 *Indra*

3 *Guru*

4 *Yama*

5 *Rudra*

6 *Brahma*

7 *Kala*

8 *Uma*

9 *Urip*

to the prescriptions of the *Asta Kosali* is always dangerous and typically involves the contraction of some awful disease, death by accident or murder, an unfaithful spouse, poverty, and the loss of the affection of the gods. These are indeed dire consequences and any mistakes in the process of construction must be carefully rectified in the prescribed manner in order to avert ill effects. Conversely, good fortune and prosperity will come to those who stick closely to the regulations. These benefits include the accumulation of wealth in the form of gold and silver, good family health, a faithful wife, loving children, and loyal servants.

BELOW LEFT TO RIGHT **Bamboo poles are the most basic building material In Bali. Bamboo has a tensile strength close to steel, but is more easily worked and far less expensive. When treated and maintained well, it can last for decades. Thatched roofs are made by tying long strands of** *alang-alang* **grass to the midribs of coconut palm fronds then lashing them to a bamboo frame using rattan cords or ties made from** *ijuk***, the fibers of the sugar palm tree. The thatch is then combed with a special rake and cut with a knife. Such roofs can last eight to ten years before needing replacement.**

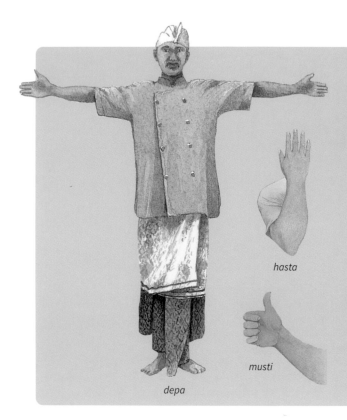

hasta

musti

depa

Applying Measurements

Having established standard units of measurement, the *Asta Kosali* then describes how they should be applied. For example, the dimensions of house posts are based on those of the hand. The ideal width for an upright is equivalent to five knuckles, identified as the sign of the "five Brahmans" (Hindu priests) and considered to have religious significance. Height is based on a composite measurement derived from the length of the index finger (*rahi*) and the gap between the second and third joints of the same digit (*guli madu*). The exact measurement is decided according to skin wrinkles and the width of the little finger (*anyari kacing*). These measurements are recorded on a bamboo stick for the use of the house builder.

Most of the rules have to do with the size and proportion of individual buildings and their relationship to one another in terms of the distance between them and their positioning inside the residential compound.

These regulations extend to the internal dimensions of a building: room sizes, thickness of walls, and so forth. Some measurements have both good and bad connotations requiring difficult choices on the part of the house builder. For example, the unit of measurement known as *patokan tujuh rasa* will encourage the accumulation of material wealth but is also likely to foster disobedient and ill-mannered children.

The Human Body as a Ruler

In many Indonesian societies, the human body provides a metaphorical model for representing the divisions of space within the house. In the Balinese residential compound, the family shrine is identified with the head; the sleeping quarters and pavilion for receiving guests with the arms; the central courtyard with the navel; the hearth with the sexual organs; the kitchen and granary with the legs and feet; and the refuse pit in the backyard with the anus.

This anthropocentric frame of reference extends to units of body measurement based on those of the house owner. These standard measurements are used to determine both the size and position of a building within the residential compound and also to calculate the dimensions of individual structural elements. Each measurement has a specific name and symbolic significance attached to its use.

The basic unit of measurement is called *depa asta musti*, which is a combination of the distance between the tip of the middle finger of each hand when the arms are stretched out horizontally on either side of the body (*depa*), plus the distance from the elbow to the tip of the middle finger (*hasta*), plus the width of the fist with the thumb extended (*musti*).

These dimensions are recorded on a length of bamboo, which serves as a kind of yardstick for laying out the compound and its buildings.

Other critical units of measurement include the span of an outstretched hand from the thumb to the tip of the little finger (*lengkat*), and the width of a closed hand with the thumb placed over the first finger (*a musti*). The Balinese also measure in feet, both lengthways (*tampak*) and by width (*tampak ngandang*).

Mantras

House building must be ritually sanctioned by the gods. Before work is begun on construction, offerings must be made on an appropriately auspicious day determined from the Balinese calendar. Ritual observations accompany each stage of construction, and the cycle is completed by a final ceremony, the *melepas*, which spiritually brings the building to life.

The *Asta Kosali* prescribes the type of mantra, or incantation, that should be recited to accompany each stage of the construction process. Particular attention is paid to the process of selecting the timber. These are the lengthiest mantras and involve descriptions of all the types of trees that may be employed for building, while invoking the blessings of the many gods and spirits associated with trees and forests, the earth and the sky. There are also mantras to bless the plot of

land prior to commencing building. These praise the major Hindu deities of the Balinese pantheon. Special attention is paid to the blessing of holy water used in the consecration of the site.

The recitation of mantras is usually accompanied by a litany of all the dangers and misfortunes associated with incorrectly carrying out the prescribed procedures. It goes without saying that neither the rituals nor the construction of the building itself can be effectively conducted by those whose thoughts are less than pure.

LEFT **The roofs of temple pagodas like this one in Ubud are made of** *ijuk*—**black fibers from the trunks of arenga sugar palm trees. These are collected, tied and cut to form interesting shapes.**

ABOVE **A Balinese family sits in front of their newly-completed house. Traditional Balinese homes consist of several small buildings and pavilions placed around a walled compound; each structure in the compound has a specific function.**

Architecture and Social Status

Balinese domestic architecture is closely linked to notions of rank and social status, with different rules and building regulations prescribed for different classes of people. Caste plays a central role, being the ultimate determinant of an individual's status in the social hierarchy, irrespective of wealth or personal achievement.

Bali's caste system has its origins in ancient India, but time and local circumstances have endowed it with a uniquely Balinese character. There are four basic divisions of society: three noble castes, collectively named *triwangsa*, and beneath them the commoners (*sudra*). The *triwangsa* are subdivided into the princely caste of royalty and warriors (*satriya*), priests (*brahmana*), and merchants (*wesia*). Rank is signalled by the use of titles, and there are subtle distinctions of status within each caste, based on genealogical descent. For instance, Balinese royalty and other members of the princely *satriya* caste like to trace their family origins back to the 14th century when Javanese colonizers first established themselves as the ruling elite in Bali following the Majapahit conquest of the island. Prominent *brahmana* families, on the other hand, claim their descent from the famous Javanese priest Danghyang Nirartha, who was responsible for a revival of Hinduism in Bali in the mid-16th century. Social interactions between the castes are fixed by conventions of speech and habit. There are three main linguistic forms in Bali: high (*alus*), middle (*madia*), and low (*kasar*) Balinese, used according to the relative status of the interlocutors.

A Matter of Proportion
The dimensions of a residential compound are carefully determined according to the owner's caste. Size matters less than proportion. Only a *raja* may erect a square or nearly square compound where the difference in length between two sides is less than one unit of measurement. The merchant caste may build nearly square compounds, so long as the difference in the length of the sides is more than two, but less than four, units. Village headmen, however, need to allow for a difference of three units between the two sides. Regulations like these cover every social category or caste affiliation.

The main units of measurement (page 12) are *depa* (the distance from fingertip to fingertip when one's arms are held out horizontally on either side of the body), *hasta* (the length of the hand measure from the elbow to the tip of the index finger), and *a musti* (the width of the closed hand with the thumb placed on top). Differences in rank and social status are reflected in different combinations of these basic units of measurement. There are three main categories: grand (*agung*) or best (*utama*); intermediate (*tengah*); and low (*rendah*). Measurements involving the third, or "sweet," finger (*jari manis*), for example, typically belong to the *agung* scheme of things. *Agung* and *utama* dimensions are much the same in terms of the actual measurements employed, but are distinguished by social evaluation: *utama* specifications are used for the houses of the wealthy, whereas only members of the aristocracy are entitled to use *agung* dimensions. Significantly, the

Asta Kosali only prescribes the minimum dimensions of a structure, which means that the compound of a commoner may actually be larger, if he can afford it, than that of an aristocrat.

FACING PAGE **A pavilion in the Ubud Royal Palace.**

ABOVE **A courtyard within the Puri Saren Agung royal palace compound in Ubud, with several small pavilions that are mainly used on ritual and festive occasions.**

From Pekarangan to Puri

The humblest type of compound, in terms of status, is that of the common man (*sudra*). This compound is called a *pekarangan* ("enclosure"). Its basic structures include a place for sleeping (*meten*); various pavilions (*bale*) for daily activities and for receiving guests; a rice granary (*lumbung*); and a cookhouse (*paon*). These are arranged around a clear central area (*natar*). The most auspicious (*kaja-kangin*) corner of the enclosure is reserved for the household temple (*sanggah*) which contains the shrines dedicated to ancestors.

The residential compounds of the three high castes are built using the same principles as the common man's but their proportions and degree of elaboration will differ. The simplest type is the *jero*, which is very similar to the *pekarangan*. The main difference is that members of the *triwangsa* castes are allowed to erect a *bale*

Gateways

In terms of the degree of ornamentation and elaboration, there is little to distinguish the entrance to the compound of a commoner from that of a nobleman, although in the case of royal palaces the main gateways to palace precincts are remarkable for their rich sculptures and ornate profile, which in many respects echo the entrances to temples. The example here is from the royal palace at Amlapura, formerly known as Karangasem.

gede—a rather grand, open-sided pavilion whose roof is supported by twelve posts—whereas commoners may not. The *bale gede* has many uses: women weave there, artisans practice their craft, children play there when it rains, and people sleep in it at night. The *bale gede* also has an important role in family rites of passage.

Another type of pavilion, called a *bale dwaja* ("flag pavilion"), is reserved for members of the princely *satri-ya* caste, while the *bale lembu-gaja*h pavilion (literally, "cow-elephant pavilion") is deemed especially suitable for the home of a Hindu or Buddhist priest.

ABOVE LEFT **The entrance gate to the temple compound in the Puri Saren Agung palace in Ubud.**

TOP **A pond and pavilion inside Puri Lukisan Art Museum in Ubud, which was constructed in the 1950s to resemble the interior of a royal Balinese palace.**

ABOVE **Ornately carved doors and doorways in the Ubud palace.**

The Bale Gede ("Great Pavilion")

Only members of the three aristocratic castes (*triwangsa*) in Bali are entitled to build themselves a *bale gede*. It is an almost square building located on the eastern side of the compound, just below the enclosure for the family shrines. Twelve posts, often built of jackfruit timber or teak, support the roof and there may also be a couple of wooden platforms at the back for sitting or sleeping on.

Typically, the *gede* is an open-sided structure with only a partial wall or wooden screens at the back of the wooden platforms. It is the only building in the compound, other than the family shrines, to have a pointed roof, all the other roofs being hipped. A pointed roof is associated with the idea of sacredness.

The *bale gede* may be used for a number of activities. It is a place where women weavers set up their looms, where artisans practise their craft, where children play when it rains, and where people sleep at night. It also plays an important role in family rites of passage. These include the celebrations held 40 days after the birth of a child, the tooth-filing ceremonies for young girls, and marriage rites. The *bale gede* is also the place where the corpse is laid out following a death in the family. Considered a living organism, the *bale* is accorded consecration rites.

ABOVE **The coronation of the king and queen of Kerambitan in Tabanan, western Bali, held in the** *bale gede* **pavilion of the palace and officiated by a** *pedanda* **or Balinese high priest.**

RIGHT **A gamelan orchestra performs during the Kerambitan coronation ceremony in a smaller pavilion near the** *bale gede* **that is set aside for this purpose.**

Priests and Princes

Jero and *pekarangan* consist of single courtyards or dwelling compounds but a Brahman who becomes a priest (*pedanda*) is entitled to a more elaborate residence (*grya*) with internal courtyards or divisions. The palace precincts (*puri*) of a royal family will be similarly subdivided into courtyards, each with specific uses relating to royal duties or prerogatives. Nevertheless, the same basic architectural principles still apply as far as orientation and the hierarchical organization of space according to the Balinese compass rose are concerned, so that one can discern a common conceptual unity linking the humblest *pekarangan* with the grandest palace.

Materials and Construction Techniques

The structure of Balinese buildings parallels the local *tri angga* classification system, which assumes that everything in the natural world can be divided into the three components of *nista*, *madya*, and *utama* (page 6). These categories are hierarchically ordered in terms of a set of spatial coordinates (high, middle, and low) identified with the base (*nista*), the house posts and curtain walls (*madya*), and the roof (*utama*).

The Base

The base, or stereobate, typically consists of four low walls of brick or stone, infilled with stamped earth. In unimportant or humble buildings, this packed earth surface will also form the material for the floor, but where finances allow, it will be paved. Similarly, the walls of the base may be plain, profiled, or carved with reliefs depending on the nature of the building and the status and wealth of the owner.

The Timber Frame

The main load-bearing elements of the building consist of a timber post-and-beam framework. This structure supports the hipped roof, which is formed from a coconut wood and bamboo frame covered with grass thatch (*alang-alang*) or, in more affluent households, with clay tiles.

The height of the posts (*adegan*) is determined by measurements taken from the house owner's body, and the dimensions of the house posts, in turn, determine the proportions of the building. The standard unit of measurement for house posts is a *rahi*, the length of a line drawn between the end of the lifeline at the base of the thumb and the tip of the index finger. Optimal heights are 20, 21, or 22 *rahi*.

A measurement of 19 *rahi* is expressly avoided, the explanation being that it would expose the occupants of the house to disease, crime, and other misfortunes. The latter measurement is sometimes referred to as *buta dengan milara* and is said to be the cause of unhappy love affairs.

The posts of the house rest on masonry or stone column bases called *umpak*, and the rigidity of the structure is established by tie-beams which are stiffened at

Movement to the Right

The first post to be erected should be the one that stands at the *kaja-kangin* corner of the building, the most auspicious position in terms of the Balinese compass rose. An offering platform is attached near the top of this post, and the erection of the rest of the posts is determined by the law of "movement to the right," an idea found all over Indonesia. In the case of Bali, this means in a clockwise direction.

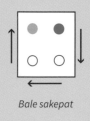

Bale sakepat

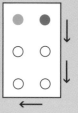

Bale sakenam

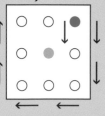

Bale tiang sanga

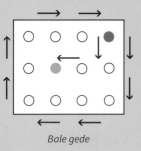

Bale gede

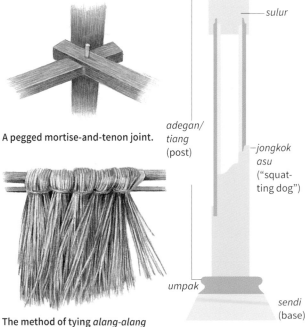

Traditional Balinese houses are built almost entirely of organic materials: wood, bamboo, grass thatch, and plant fibers.

A pegged mortise-and-tenon joint.

The method of tying *alang-alang* thatch.

sulur

adegan/ tiang (post)

—jongkok asu ("squatting dog")

umpak

sendi (base)

The parts of a house post.

the joints by shores or brackets. Individual components are joined by mortise-and-tenon, or lap joints, and are secured by a wedge or wooden peg.

The *Asta Kosali* prescribes what kinds of timber should be used for particular building requirements. Traditionally, the preferred material for house posts is teak, which ideally should be cut from a living tree growing locally, although teak imported from Kalimantan or Java is considered to be superior.

Offerings must be made before the tree is felled and, when the posts are ready to be raised into position, care must be taken to ensure that they are erected according to the direction of growth of the tree trunk from which they were cut, with the root end being placed in the foundations and the growing tip end supporting the roof. On no account may posts be erected "upside down," that is to say, with the direction of growth inverted.

The Walls

The walls of Balinese houses are made from stone, brick, or even simply mud. They do not carry any load, as they are completely detached from the timber structure that supports the roof.

The favored building material is *paras*, a kind of soft sandstone that is cut into uniform brick-sized blocks and then gently baked in the sun. Using muddy water for mortar, these bricks are rubbed back and forth on the preceding course until they stick. When the mud is still wet, it provides an element of adhesion. Subsequently, the wall is held together simply by its weight and the near-perfect fit between courses. *Paras* is a very plastic material, which can be easily carved, but is not very durable and soon deteriorates when exposed to the elements, hence the ancient appearance of many Bali-

ABOVE AND LEFT **Walls and pillars in Bali are usually made of soft and porous fired clay bricks. Once cemented in place, the surfaces of the bricks are ground so the seams between the bricks disappear and the surfaces becomes quite smooth. Concrete bricks are also commonly in use today. Much of the work of carrying the materials is done by women, whereas the bricklaying and sanding is done by men. Packed clay walls are still used for the outer walls of village homes. Old brick walls and foundations eventually become covered in moss and lichen in the humid climate, which makes them appear "alive."**

nese buildings, despite the fact that most structures are no more than a few years old.

The Balinese also employ adobe as a building material. This is made locally from wet earth kneaded into balls and placed in the sun to dry.

Walls are constructed by placing these mud balls in parallel rows and then filling the crevices with more mud. Another layer is added on top, and the process is repeated until the desired wall elevation is achieved.

Adobe is even less durable than *paras*. As such, it always has a protective coping of thatch that is usually made from rice straw. Rice straw thatch does not itself last very long and is usually renewed after each harvest.

The Roof

Since the materials used to make walls are not very durable, care is taken to ensure that the walls are well protected from the elements by widely overhanging eaves. The main framework is made of bamboo with the roof ridge supported by king posts, girders, and columns.

The usual roofing material used in ordinary buildings is a thick thatch that is made from *alang-alang grass (Imperata cylindrica)*. The grass is gathered in bundles which are then doubled over the midrib of coconut fronds and stitched in place. These sections of thatching are lashed on to the bamboo framework of

the roof using red-dyed rattan cords or ties made from the natural fiber of the sugar palm (*Arenga pinnata*). Extra thatch is placed along the ridges for reinforcement. Lastly, the roof is combed with a special type of rake and the bottom edge is trimmed with a knife. Such a roof, which may be up to 50 centimeters in thickness, can last for many years.

More important structures may employ locally made clay pantiles, or even modern Marseilles tiles, while split bamboo shingles are a popular choice for roofing material in mountain regions as they are more durable than thatch. In the case of religious structures and family shrines, black thatch (*ijuk*) from the sugar palm is used for roofing instead of *alang-alang*.

Ornamentation and Iconography

Balinese temples are enlivened by a variety of stone sculptures and reliefs, which to the Western eye have an almost baroque or rococo quality. The original inspiration for many of the statues and motifs may have come from India, but everywhere they have been subjected to strong local influences, which over centuries have given rise to a uniquely Balinese artistic tradition.

The basic material used for stone carving is a soft volcanic sandstone, or tuff, called *paras*, which is quarried from riverbanks in central and coastal Bali. It has a very plastic quality and lends itself well to being shaped by the stonemason's chisel for courtyard walls, temple gates, shrines, and especially for the ubiquitous statuary for which Bali is so famous. Equally, *paras* deteriorates fairly rapidly when exposed to the elements, and for this reason Balinese temples and other structures are in a constant process of renovation and renewal. Works of art rarely survive beyond 100 years and it is not common for a temple's shrine, gates, and walls to be reconstructed and recarved every 30 years.

ABOVE **Like other Balinese structures, the dimensions of an entrance are endowed with symbolic or ritual significance linked to the unit of measurement used in setting it out, the type of ritual employed in its consecration, and the particular deity—for example, Mahadewi, Saraswati, or Dewi Sri—to whom it is dedicated. There are places for offerings on either side of the entrance. These may either be a pair of niches in the external wall or two free-standing offering columns (*apit lawang*) on either side of the doorway.**

LEFT **This Bhoma head is from Desa Pakudi, Gianyar. The image is clearly related to the *kala* heads that are found over the doorways of Javanese temples dating from the classical era of Indonesia's Hindu-Buddhist past.**

A Balinese Iconography

One of the most striking images in Balinese temples is the face of a leering monster, with lolling tongue, bulging eyes, and ferociously large canines, which is typically found over the monumental gateway (*kori agung*) leading to the innermost courtyard. This demonic visage is the face of the popular Hindu god Bhoma (the protector), son of Durga and Siwa (the destroyer), whose fearful, yet strangely benevolent, countenance is intended to drive away malevolent influences from the temple precincts. Throughout the island, Bhoma is found carved into brick, shaped out of *paras*, and, in some cases, merely painted on to walls over doorways.

Corner motifs include *karang curing*, which are composed of the upper part of a bird's beak with a single eye and jagged teeth, or as an alternative, *karang asti*, the jawless head of an elephant. When the Mexican artist and author Miguel Covarrubias, who lived in Bali during the 1930s, asked why these images lacked a lower mandible, he was told that this was because they did not have to eat solid food.

Other decorative motifs include border designs (*patra*), of which there are several kinds. The type

A Rich Stone Carving Tradition

The most ornately carved structures in Bali are located along the northern coast. Balinese rococo flourished here, in contrast to the more stolid and stately Majapahit styles commonly associated with the south. Each region had—and still has—its unique carving style. Likewise, certain materials are associated with certain areas. Split metamorphic rock, found in the vicinity of volcanic eruptions, is widely used in the mountains, along the northern coast, and in the east. Cement moldings as decorative trim are a feature of eastern Bali, while plaster walls decorated with bas-reliefs fashioned from cement are popular on the north coast. Tiered baked clay bricks (*bata bali*), carved with decorative panels, are used for courtyard walls, gates, and shrines all over the island. However, it is the combination of restrained *bata bali* architecture and florid *paras* ornamentation—a purely Balinese invention—that distinguishes the island's decorative tradition from any other.

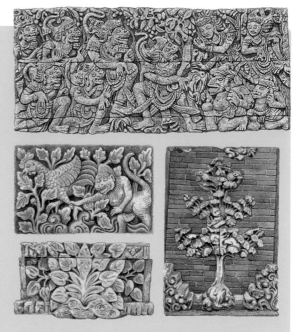

TOP RIGHT **Relief depicting a scene from the *Ramayana*, Desa Kaba-kaba, Tabanan. Rama and Laksamana are in the top right-hand corner, while Hanuman and his monkey army approach from the left.**

MIDDLE LEFT **Comic relief from Sibang Gede, Tabanan. A mischievous monkey catches a chicken by the foot.**

ABOVE **Typical foliate decorative element, Desa Sebatu, Gianyar.**

ABOVE RIGHT ***Paras* floral carving on a red brick base, Taman Pura Puleh, Mas.**

A whimsical modern stone carving of a man surrounded by floral motifs who almost seems to be riding a bicycle (although the handlebars are missing!).

known as *patra olanda* might have been inspired by Dutch sources, while the pattern *patra cina* indicates Chinese origins. Lotus petals and swastika, the latter the symbol of Hindu Bali, are particularly propitious motifs.

Padmasana shrines and *meru* are typically decorated with geometric or foliate motifs, while the carvings on pavilions may include representations of animals and mythological beasts, such as winged lions (*singa*) and *garuda* birds or even the gods themselves.

The most important carved images, however, are reserved for the walls and gateways of temples for they divide the sacred precincts of the temple from the profane, secular world outside. Especially significant are the reliefs which adorn the free-standing brick or stone wall, the *aling-aling*, which is placed just behind the *kori agung* gateway as one enters the innermost courtyard in the temple complex. The latter typically sports a rogues' gallery of demons and ogres who are intended to deter malevolent influences from penetrating the inner sanctum.

ABOVE Carved stone statues of characters from the Indian Mahabharata epic stand in ponds of holy water from a sacred spring located within the Tirta Gangga ("Ganges Water") Water Palace in Karangasem, in eastern Bali.

LEFT Images of the legendary white monkey, Hanuman, are common in the Balinese iconographic repertoire. Hanuman features prominently in the *Ramayana* as the general of the monkey army which helped Rama and Laksamana recapture the former's wife Sita from the devilish Rawana, King of Sri Lanka, who had abducted her.

ABOVE A temple guardian stands outside the main shrine of the Gunung Kawi Sebatu temple and bathing complex in central Bali.

Bali Aga Mountain Architecture

The people who live in the mountains of central Bali, the Bali Aga, are rather different from other Balinese—it is often implied that they represent what the Balinese were like before the arrival of Hindu and Buddhist influences from India and Java—and therefore they possess different cultural and architectural traditions.

Although many people believe that the Bali Aga represent a kind of ancestral population, many of the Bali Aga's cultural traditions are clearly related to those of their lowland cousins. Nevertheless, the Bali Aga have exercised an independent existence since the earliest times; many of the edicts of the first Hindu-Buddhist kings of Bali, in the 10th century, were addressed to the village communities classified today as Bali Aga.

The principal point of divergence between lowland and mountain Balinese seems to have been the resistance of the latter to Majapahit influences from the 14th century onward: the Bali Aga people do not cremate their dead, they are not organized into castes, and so forth. Naturally, their remote location in the clefts of mountain valleys, has played a big part in helping the Bali Aga to retain their cultural and political autonomy. This isolation has also meant that they have retained more of their Austronesian cultural heritage than their lowland neighbors, who came under the influence of the Hindu courts established by Javanese princes and Majapahit settlers.

Village Layout

The Bali Aga villages are spatially oriented along the same lines as those in the lowlands, being laid out in relation to a mountain-sea axis (*kaja-kelod*) and the path of the sun. In other respects, however, they are quite different. Although the Bali Aga live in extended family compounds called *banjaran* or *pekarangan*, which are enclosed by an earthen wall or hedge, the individual, thatch-covered structures within the compound are not functionally differentiated and each building constitutes a self-contained unit which is home to a married couple, their children, and sometimes an elderly, dependent parent. These quite separate households are called *kuren*, which is the common term for both a hearth and the group of people who share the food cooked on it. *Kuren* represent the basic social and economic unit of Bali Aga society. The heart of a Bali Aga village is the *bale agung*, the sacred council house.

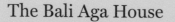

The Bali Aga House

The Bali Aga house is a rectangular post-and-beam structure supporting a steeply pitched roof made of bamboo shingles or of a thick grass thatch. It is raised on a low plinth of compacted earth, faced with stone, and the walls are typically thick wooden planks or plaited bamboo strips. The windows, if they occur at all, are small. A single door faces the center of the compound.

As with the lowland Balinese, house dimensions are based on bodily measurements taken from the male head of the household. One feature that distinguishes Bali Aga architecture from that of the lowlands is the division of the interior of the house into male and female spaces. The uphill (*kaja*) end of the house is for men—it is where they sit when they are inside—while women are linked with the downhill (*kelod*) end of the house, where food is prepared and stored and children are cared for.

Compound Layout

The individual houses within a compound are arranged in broad rows or avenues along an uphill-downhill axis, with the most senior member of the extended family occupying the house at the uphill (*kaja*) end of the compound. A single row of houses indicates a compound established by just one male ancestor.

As the male children of a Bali Aga couple marry and form their own households, new houses are added at the downhill end of the row. At the same time, however, as older generations of Bali Aga die, the houses that they occupied at the uphill end of the compound become vacant and are inherited by younger married couples, rather like a game of musical chairs, or if there are no heirs, are returned to the village. In this respect, residence patterns within the family compound reflect the relative status of different households within the extended family group.

Sometimes one finds two rows of houses laid out in parallel within a single compound, which indicates that the family compound was established by more than one founder, perhaps by a pair of brothers, for example, or by brothers-in-law. In this case, the entrances of the houses all face inward, toward the center line of the compound, with the layout of the houses in the left and right rows reversed.

Each compound contains an origin temple (*kemulan*) at the sacred, uphill (*kaja*) end, dedicated to the ancestors of the extended family who reside there.

Bali Aga villages, of which a number may be found throughout the mountains around Kintamani in central Bali, are clearly distinguished by their unusual layout

The Bale Agung

A distinctive feature of Bali Aga society is the council of elders, which presides over community affairs. Its members represent individual households and are the most senior married men in the village. When a member dies or steps down, his place is taken by his eldest married son or the next youngest married man in the village. The council meets periodically to discuss community affairs. Each village has a great hall, or *bale agung*, where they assemble. This is an elongated platform, rather like an open-sided cattle shed, but raised on a masonry plinth. Council members sit according to their status in the community, with the most senior members at the uphill (*kaja*) end of the building. In the same way that residence patterns within the family compound reflect the status of the individual households, the overall seating plan in the *bale agung* quite literally maps out the local social hierarchy on the ground.

and the uniformity of the houses; it is as if they all adhere to a single design. However, traditional Bali Aga architecture is disappearing in many places as houses are being rebuilt using modern materials.

Pura Penulisan

The temple complex at Pura Penulisan has been an important center of Bali Aga worship since earliest times. Perched high (1745 meters) on the ring of mountains that surrounds Mt. Batur, the series of ascending terraces recalls similar prehistoric sites in other parts of the Indonesian archipelago. The earliest inscriptions, written in an ancient Javanese script, date from the 11th century and relate to a number of male and female statues on the uppermost terrace, generally assumed to be portraits of royalty. Their presence may indicate the existence of an ancestral cult of divine rulers similar to the god-kings (*devaraja*) of Angkor Wat in Cambodia.

*Pura Sakawana
Penulisan*

The Heritage of Majapahit

The temples of Bali are the legacy, in part, of an architectural tradition dating back to the East Javanese kingdom of Majapahit, which held sway over most of the archipelago in the 14th and 15th centuries. Construction techniques employed by the ancient Javanese are still used today in Bali, and many architectural elements—most notably the distinctive split gateway—can be traced back to the golden Majapahit era.

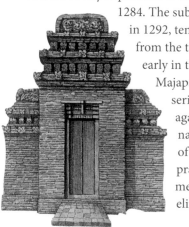

Bali first came under the hegemony of Java in the latter part of the 13th century when the last ruler of Singasari, the dynasty which preceded Majapahit in East Java, sent a military expedition to subjugate the island in 1284. The subsequent fall of Singasari, in 1292, temporarily released Bali from the thrall of East Java, but early in the 14th century, the new Majapahit rulers conducted a series of military campaigns against Bali which culminated in the installation of a Javanese king at Samprangan and the establishment of a Javanese ruling elite across the island.

The end of the 15th century saw a gradual decline in Majapahit fortunes as autonomous Muslim entrepot states began to establish themselves along the northern coastline of Java. The final collapse of this last great empire of Indonesia's Hindu-Buddhist past came at the beginning of the 16th century, and led to a huge influx of Javanese refugees into Bali.

Among them were Javanese nobles and courtiers, as well as many artists and artisans who had formerly

ABOVE **The spectacular entrance gate to Pura Bukit Dharma in Buruan village, near Gianyar and Goa Gajah. Although the construction is modern, it echoes the ancient Majapahit construction and design with red brick walls and carved *paras* (volcanic tuff) ornamentations.**

LEFT **The *kori agung* gateway of Pura Maospahit is built in the Majapahit style. Some of the earliest parts of the complex may date back to that era.**

been employed at the Majapahit court. This event had a lasting impact on the religious and cultural life of the island: these refugees brought not only their caste system and a variety of ceremonies and dances with them but also introduced new elements into Balinese temple architecture.

Majapahit Correspondences

The ruined temples of East Java reveal that the religious orientation of the Majapahit era was predominantly Hindu, but with a sizable Buddhist constituency. This same combination of Sivaitic Hinduism and Buddhism occurs in Bali, except that the relationship between Hinduism and Buddhism is more syncretic in nature, with Hinduism grabbing the higher ground though itself greatly modified by native Balinese influences. Nevertheless, a number of parallels with the Majapahit era can still be drawn. For example, the Balinese continue to cremate their dead and cast their ashes upon the sea. Like the ancient Javanese, they also conduct a series of post-mortem rituals to free the soul from the pollution of death.

One major difference between modern Bali and Majapahit Java is the absence of a physical representa-

Pura Maospahit in Denpasar is constructed of red fired bricks in the ancient East Javanese style.

tion of the deity in Bali, except in the case of a few pre-Majapahit era temples of great antiquity.

The temple complex at Pura Sada Kapal is surrounded by a wall of red brick constructed in the traditional way without mortar. By rubbing one stone against the other, a fine powder crumbles from the surface layers. When water is added to it, the stones can simply be stuck together.

The Pura Sada Kapal Sanctuary

The Pura Sada at Kapal is the oldest dynastic temple in the former kingdom of Mengwi and exemplifies the "Majapahit" style of architecture. The sanctuary was almost completely destroyed by a severe earthquake in 1917, but was restored with the help of the Archeological Service in 1949–50 in the East Javanese style of the original.

The temple complex is surrounded by a red brick wall built in the traditional way. The beautiful split gate leading to the spacious first courtyard is one of the temple's few earlier structures. Although badly cracked in the earthquake, it has been successfully restored. In the first courtyard is a handsome pavilion where visiting deities gather to converse through trance mediums during the temple's anniversary. However, the most important structure inside the temple precincts, located in the inner courtyard, is an 11-tiered tower, or *prasada*, of red brick dedicated to the royal family of Mengwi's deified ancestors. Behind the *prasada*, standing on a low plinth, is a curious arrangement of 54 stone seats with three larger ones facing them. The story behind them relates how the cremated remains of one of the rulers of Majapahit were carried down to the sea by 54 of his followers and their three leaders, to be cast to the ocean waves, as still occurs in contemporary Balinese mortuary rites. The ashes, together with a bamboo funerary tower, were placed in a small boat (*kapal*) and the party set out from the shore. Unfortunately, they ended up stranded at sea, but their ill-fated voyage has become immortalized in the serried ranks of stone seats and the *prasada* (which represents the bamboo funerary tower) at the Pura Sada Kapal.

Nirartha: Bali's Master Builder

The promulgation of Hindu and Buddhist doctrines in Bali is attributed to a number of key historical figures, typically Brahman priests from Java and their disciples or descendants. A famous early example is the 11th-century reformer, Mpu Kuturan, but perhaps the most renowned of all is the 16th-century Javanese priest, Danghyang Dwijendra, otherwise known as Nirartha.

Nirartha came to Bali from Kediri in East Java, in 1537, in the aftermath of the collapse of the Majapahit empire. Legend has it that he made the crossing from Java on a leaf of the *keluwih* tree. Upon landing near Negara in the kingdom of Jembrana, he sat down to rest under an *ancak* tree, a relative of the banyan under which the Buddha famously meditated. His followers subsequently built a temple on the site, the Pura Ancak, today's Pura Prancak.

Nirartha was invited to settle in Mas by a local prince, Mas Wilis. However, news of his teachings soon reached the ascendant royal house of Gelgel, and an emissary was dispatched to bring the Pedanda Sakti Wauh Ruah, or "Newly Arrived Magically Powerful High Priest," to the court.

Once installed at the palace of Gelgel, Nirartha concentrated on matters of ritual practice, especially those connected with marriage, pregnancy, childbirth, death and the postmortem purification of the soul. He still found time, however, to embark upon several missionary journeys through Bali, Lombok, and Sumbawa. During his travels he founded many temples, while the children of his several marriages, both in Java and in Bali, became the progenitors of important Brahman clans, whose descendants still rank among the most important *brahmana* families in Bali today.

OPPOSITE LEFT Niche with statue, Pura Taman Puleh, Mas.

BELOW Pura Taman Pule, in the village of Mas, some 20 kilometers to the north of Denpasar on the road to Ubud, is historically famous for having been the site of the hermitage of Nirartha. It is said that some of Nirartha's personal relics are hidden here.

Nirartha's Temple Building

Between 1546 and 1550, Danghyang Nirartha traveled all over Bali, teaching as he went and founding temples along the way. The famous temple of Tanah Lot, in the former kingdom of Tabanan, is one such sanctuary. It is said that on one of Nirartha's journeys round Bali, he chose to sleep at this unusual rocky outcrop on the shores of the kingdom of Tambanan, and out of sheer adoration for the natural beauty of the landscape recommended that a temple be built on the site.

At Pura Taman Pule, in the center of Mas, a *padmasana* surrounded by a pond is said to have been the site of Danghyang Nirartha's original home. The delicate leaf-shaped inner gate at the temple is reminiscent of a *kayonan*, the shadow puppet representing the tree of life or sacred mountain, universal nature, and the gateway to the world beyond. People from all over Bali come to pray at this auspicious temple.

ABOVE RIGHT **Pura Tanah Lot in southwest Bali is one of the island's most famous sights. The temple perches on a jagged outcropping of rock that is lashed by waves from the Southern Ocean. Danghyang Nirartha is said to have recommended that this temple be built here due to its dramatic location. It is one of the Sad Kahyangan or six cardinal sanctuaries on Bali.**

RIGHT **Pura Goa Lawah, the "Bat Cave Temple" in eastern Bali is said to have been established in the 11th century by Mpu Kuturan, another Javanese priest who arrived centuries before Nirartha to spread the Hindu-Javanese religion in Bali.**

A Passion for Padmasana

As well as founding new temples, Danghyang Nirartha also encouraged the building of *padmasana* at many of the existing temples he visited. These he dedicated to Ida Sanghyang Widhi Wasa, the Supreme Being or Ultimate Godhead. The *padmasana* at the Pura Kehen in Bangli (right) rests on top of a stone turtle, which represents the mythical earth-supporting chelonian, Bedawang Nala. The two serpents coiled around Bedawang Nala's body are said to stand for man's earthly needs. The last *padmasana* to be built by Danghyang Nirartha was at Pura Luhur Uluwatu on the westernmost tip of the Bukit Peninsula (pages 68–71). It was here that he achieved his apotheosis, or liberation (*moksa*), from the endless cycle of rebirth, becoming one with the infinite.

Ancient Cave Temples & Rock-cut Sanctuaries

As in India, some of the earliest surviving sanctuaries in Bali have been hewn directly from a rock face, the best known of these being Gunung Kawi and Goa Gajah. Both sanctuaries are to be found in the vicinity of Gianyar, in the narrow strip of land lying between the Petanu and Pakerisan rivers. This is a region which is extraordinarily rich in ancient temple sites and sanctuaries.

Gunung Kawi, located just near the source of the Pakerisan River, about halfway up Mt. Batur, literally means "Mountain of the Poet(s)," the poet in this case being none other than the god Siwa. In the ravines on both sides of the river, royal "tombs," a hermitage, and monks' caves have been cut out of solid rock. The main monument consists of a series of temple-like structures, standing in two rows and excavated directly from the rock face. Though no more than deeply-cut reliefs, in form they resemble classical Javanese temples, or *candi*, with their stepped pyramidal roofs and serried ranks of antefixes, but their "doors" do not open and there are no internal spaces. The oval-roofed

niches are each about 7 meters high. The reliefs are covered with a type of plaster. On the other side of the ravine are five similar niches.

The temple-like niches are undoubtedly commemorative structures, as there are inscriptions over the false doorways indicating to whom they are dedicated. The latter are executed in a highly decorative script, sometimes known as "Kadiri Quadrate" after the East Javanese kingdom of Kadiri where it is also found in the late 10th and 11th centuries. Unfortunately, the inscriptions are badly worn and are virtually illegible except in the case of one associated with the central *candi*, which reads "*haji lumah ing Jalu*" (literally, "the king who was 'monumen-

Cloisters and Meditation Cells

Immediately south of the rock-cut niches at Gunung Kawi lies a warren of "cloisters" (*patapan*) carved into the rock face. This was the inner sanctum of priestly guardians and trance oracles, who would pass on advice to the living from the long-dead and deified king. The cloisters consist of a series of courtyards, monks' cells and meditation niches. The largest of these chambers has windows and a hole in the ceiling to admit light. There is a central dais and stone seats cut into the surrounding walls, rather like a chapter house in a medieval monastery in Europe.

OPPOSITE PAGE Dramatic Javanese-style *candi* or commemorative temples for the royal family cut from solid rock at Gunung Kawi—the "Temple of the Poets"—in central Bali. The Gunung Kawi complex consists of two rows of large rock-cut *candi* as well as a series of smaller niches, courtyards and cloisters likewise cut from the solid rock.

BELOW A moss-covered stone sculpture sits quietly in a forest near the Goa Gajah "Elephant Cave" sanctuary. This area lies between two major rivers, the Petanu and the Pekerisan, which run north-south from the mountains to the sea, and it is scattered with ancient temples and remains dating back a thousand years.

talized' at Jalu"). The king referred to here is generally thought to be the 11th-century Balinese ruler, Anak Wungsu. Known chiefly from royal proclamations carved in stone, Anak Wungsu probably ruled from about 1050 until at least 1078 (the date of his last inscription).

As kings were cremated and their ashes cast into the sea, the *candi* at Gunung Kawi contain no human remains and are not, in fact, "tombs" but symbols of the deified rulers. However, during Gunung Kawi's annual temple festival, it is believed that the royal souls still descend to take up temporary residence in the niches so that their beneficial and fertilizing powers may flow down the Pakerisan River and through the rice fields of the kingdom.

Sacred Serpents and Water

On the hillside above the group of five rock-cut *candi*, there is a conduit which carries water to a lower channel that passes right in front of the *candi* themselves. In front of each of the *candi*, there is a spout and water issues forth from these into another conduit which empties into a recessed bathing place. The spout in front of the central candi, which commemorates the deceased king, is carved in the shape of a *naga* serpent, while the other spouts are plain. *Naga* are traditionally associated with water and fertility throughout Southeast Asia, and it seems likely that in the past it was believed that immersion in water which had come into contact with the memorial to the late ruler would enhance fecundity or cure barrenness and other ills.

ABOVE **The bathing pools in front of Goa Gajah were only discovered and excavated in 1954. One side is for men, the other for women. (See page 23 for a close-up of the water spouts that are sculpted in the shape of heavenly nymphs.)**

LEFT AND BELOW **More ancient stone carvings found strewn around the Goa Gajah temple site. As with the carvings on the mouth of the cave itself, it is not clear what these represent. They include fanciful animals, snakes, monsters, goblins and phantoms as well as leaves and vines.**

Goa Gajah

The remarkable façade of the Goa Gajah or "Elephant Cave" temple has been sculpted directly from the rock face. It features monstrous creatures and the leering face of a demonic being whose mouth forms the entrance portal, no doubt designed to prevent malevolent influences from entering the sanctuary. The complex contains a T-shaped grotto, a small pavilion housing a 1,000-year-old statue of the Buddhist goddess Hariti, protector of children, and a bathing spot consisting of three sunken compartments.

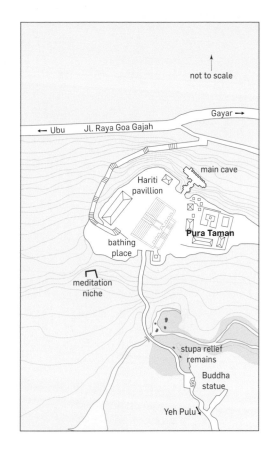

LEFT **Goa Giri Putri is a huge natural limestone cave complex on the neighboring island of Nusa Penida, immediately to the southeast of Bali. This cave is a popular pilgrimage site for Balinese who visit the temple to participate in purification rituals. The complex has six large chambers where the rituals are held.**

Balinese Palaces

In traditional Hindu cosmology, the territory of the kingdom was conceived symbolically as replicating the universe—a microcosm of the macrocosm. The seat of the ruler, who was regarded as divinely appointed in classical Indonesia, was ideally situated at or near the geographical center of the kingdom—the ultimate source of temporal power as well as a cosmological and ritual center.

Following the conquest of Bali by the East Javanese Majapahit kingdom in the early 14th century, a vassal king was installed at Samprangan, near present-day Gianyar, who owed his allegiance to Java. The island was effectively a dependency of Java until the start of the 15th century. As Majapahit fortunes waned, however, Bali gradually gained its autonomy from Java. Following the collapse of the Majapahit empire in the early years of the 16th century, Bali grew to be an imperial power in its own right under the leadership of King Waturenggong. By the end of the next century, Bali had fragmented into several lesser kingdoms. These survive today as eight regencies (*kabupaten*), Bali's local government departments. In the 16th to 19th centuries, Bali's "Golden Age," grand palaces were regarded as the physical manifestation of the popularity of the royal dynasties of Bali.

BELOW **A panoramic view of Puri Saren Agung palace in Ubud showing the open pavilions around the outer courtyard where guests may be received and performances are held on ritual days.**

Royal Entertainments

The main entrance to the palace precincts is ideally located at the *kelod* end of the complex, on the west (*kauh*) side. The courtyard is typically enclosed by a tracery wall (*ancak saji*) which gives the space an open feel. This is where the ruler meets his subjects, and where royal entertainments are held. There are usually several open pavilions for guests and one to house the gamelan, while an impressive *kori agung* gateway leading into the next courtyard provides a dramatic point of entry for performers in other court theatricals. The central courtyard at the *kelod* end of the complex is called the *samanggen* and serves as the forecourt to the *raja's* quarters (*pelataran rangki*) at the very center of the palace precincts. In the final courtyard at this end of the palace complex, where they can be entered discretely by the *raja's* staff via a screened door, are the servant's quarters, kitchen, and granary.

At the Center

The palace (*puri*) of the local dynastic ruler (*raja*) and his family was ideally located on an auspicious site, preferably within the *kaja-kangin* quadrant formed by the crossroads at the center of town. In practice, local circumstances and history often made this impossible, especially if there was more than one palace complex. At Karangasem, for example, an older palace was left by the founders of a new dynasty to senior relatives; at Bangli, where two earlier palaces occupy the center of Bangli, the principal one is situated in the *kaja-kauh* quadrant.

Palace Layout

The palace resembles the basic square grid established for the residential compound of the common man, for it is laid out according to the same rules of the Balinese compass rose and according to mandalas described in architectural manuals such as the *Asta Kosali*. For palaces, however, the division of the area enclosed by the perimeter walls is given a physical reality, with walls and doorways dividing the palace precincts into a series of interconnected courtyards.

The Dynastic Temple

The *kaja-kangin* sector of the grid is occupied, predictably, by the family temple (*pamerajan*) of the ruler, which in this instance forms a kind of cosmic center of the political territory. Unlike ordinary family temples,

The base, eaves and roof supports of pavilions in the Puri Saren Agung palace are elaborately decorated, and on festive occasions the pillars are wrapped with exquisite purple and gold fabric.

it is open to the public on ceremonial occasions and is approached from the *kauh* side of the palace complex via two intermediary courtyards (*jaba* and *jaba tengah*). The first of these is ideally situated on the western side of the palace complex and is entered from outside the palace walls via a ceremonial split gateway (*candi bentar*). The second courtyard is used for the preparation of offerings and the reception of guests attending palace ceremonies. This courtyard is completely enclosed on all sides and is entered from the outer courtyard by another ceremonial gateway called a *kori agung*, which has a lintel and doors that can be shut. The *kori agung* is usually quite an ornate structure, with statuary and carvings intended to deter malevolent influences from entering the inner sanctum of the royal temple. The

The most important of the three residential courts that occupy the central row of the palace complex is the middle one, which is where the *raja* and his family live. A wall bisects the court along an east-west axis and symbolizes the division between the public and private lives of the ruler. The *kelod* half is the public domain and is reached by the public from the *kelod* end of the palace complex. This court has a *bale gede* where important life-cycle rituals relating to members of the royal family take place, and there is also likely to be a pavilion to house important guests.

The *kaja* half of the central court is occupied by the ruler and his immediate family. The main building is the living quarters (*ukiran*) of the *raja* himself. Located exactly in the middle of the palace complex where it is divided in two by the wall that separates the central courtyard into its *kaja* and *kelod* halves, the *ukiran*'s distinguished status is signalled by its pointed roof; all other buildings have hipped roofs, except for the family shrines and the *meru* towers.

aling-aling wall inside the gateway is also decorated with reliefs, which often allude to the date of construction. The doorway in the *kori agung* is opened only on ceremonial occasions, with everyday access afforded by a smaller, less elaborate, door to one side.

The sanctum sanctorum of the royal family temple (*jero dalem*) contains the ancestral shrines of the ruling dynasty, which are much the same as other family shrines except that they are usually more numerous and more elaborately ornamented. There are also *meru* towers dedicated to the gods. The number of tiered roofs (*tumpang*) is always uneven; the exact number depends on the nature of the deity to whom the structure is dedicated and the status of the person responsible for its erection. A *raja* who dedicates a *meru* to Siwa is entitled to build the maximum number of *tumpang*—eleven.

ABOVE **An elevated and elaborately decorated pavilion in which the ruler holds ceremonial audiences and receives VIP guests.**

BELOW **A ceremonial *candi bentar* split gate (on the left) and an ornate *kulkul* bell tower (in the center), overlooking a pond strewn with water lilies.**

Prince or Commoner?

Not much distinguishes the palace of a *raja* or Balinese prince from the residential compounds of his former subjects. The main difference is their overall size—they can develop into sprawling complexes over time—the quality of the building materials, and the degree of ornamentation. Gateways, standing on the threshold of the royal precincts, provide an opportunity for impressive display of sculptured forms and other decorative elements.

Royal thrones for the ruler and his wife are draped in purple *prada* cloths (purple is the royal color), with gold foil appliqué added.

ABOVE A twin-leafed door, elaborately carved and painted in the east Bali chinoiserie style, popular throughout the 20th century. Such doors are commonly seen on the palaces in Gianyar, Karangasem and Klungkung.

Water Gardens

Water pavilions, or "floating palaces" (*bale kambang*) as they are more poetically known, occupy a special place in Balinese architecture. Traditionally associated with the ruler in Java during the Hindu-Buddhist era, the water garden seems to have been perceived in a mystical light—as a place apart from the mundane where the king could go to meditate and communicate with the gods.

TOP The vast water garden complex at Ujung in eastern Bali was completed by the last ruler of Karangasem (now called Amlapura) in 1921. It was designed by a Dutch and a Chinese architect working in tandem, and features a large pool of water near the seaside with a European-style villa at its center, connected on both sides by long bridges with lavish gardens and pavilions all around it. The water palace was completely reconstructed in the early 2000s and is open to the public.

Lovely sculptures straddle the wall lining the moat around the *Bale Kambang* "Floating Pavilion" at Klungkung (now called Semarapura)

An island at the center of a lake or pond appears to have been a typical feature of a Javanese water pavilion. This design may have originated in cosmographical terms as a representation of the Hindu-Buddhist universe with the ruler positioned at the center (Mt. Meru), his temporal powers sanctioned by the gods.

Similar ideas existed in Bali. The temple complex at Taman Ayun in the former kingdom of Mengwi is completely surrounded by a moat and was built as an earthly replica of the heavens where the deified ancestors of the royal family of Mengwi are supposed to disport themselves in floating pavilions attended to by celestial nymphs—a delightful idea and one that was replicated in the ornamental lotus pools and *bale kambang* of Balinese palaces.

The Canadian-born composer and writer Colin McPhee, who lived in Bali for several years before the Second World War, provides this atmospheric description in *A House in Bali* of his visits to the water garden in the palace compound of the impoverished Raja of Saba, in the former kingdom of Karangasem: "As our friendship grew the Anak Agung's gifts (without which I could never depart) became more personal—a ring; a handsome fighting cock; a cutting from one of his precious litchi trees. And always three or four *gurami* fish fresh from the water, still twitching on the thong that held them by the gills.

Taman SoekasadaUjung

The complex of pools and pavilions at Taman Ujung was built in 1919 by the last ruler of Karangasem, Anak Agung Angulurah Ketut, and was one of three water palaces that he built during his lifetime, the other two being at Tirta Gangga and Jungutan. Most of the lavish palace complex at Ujung—a vast pool bordered by small pavilions with a massive stained-glass and stucco bungalow in the center—was completely destroyed by the eruption of Mt. Agung in 1963 and by subsequent seismic activity. Little else but the limpid pools and lotus blossoms remained. The entire complex was rebuilt in phases between 1998 and 2004 in a project funded by the World Bank. Unusually, the bas-reliefs on the pavilions do not appear to have been carved by Balinese but instead show strong European and Chinese influences.

"These fish were fat and delicious, and were raised in an artificial pond that lay in the park beyond the palace. Once this had been a fine garden, but now hibiscus, gardenia, jasmine and poinsettia fought amongst themselves beneath the confusion of palms. Orchids drooped from boughs, and the ground was black and slippery.

LEFT ABOVE AND BELOW The magnificent *Bale Kambang*, or "Floating Pavilion" in Semarapura (formerly Klungkung), is often cited as one of the most beautiful buildings in Bali. Klungkung's kings once ruled all of Bali and this complex is all that remains of the original palace. The raised pavilion is surrounded by a lotus pond and accessed by a narrow causeway from one end. The brick walls around the pavilion and pond support elegantly-carved sculptures and the ceiling of the pavilion itself is painted with stories in the traditional Kamasan style.

BELOW The "Mahabharata Pond" at the Tirta Gangga royal water garden near Amlapura, in east Bali. The pond is fed by a sacred spring and the water is believed to have healing powers. The pleasure garden was built as a royal retreat by the ruler of Karangasem in 1948 then destroyed by the eruption of Mt. Agung in 1963. The water garden (but not the buildings) have since been completely reconstructed including the stone sculptures of characters from the Mahabharata epic, all of which are new.

The pond had a little pleasure pavilion in the center, connected to the land by a rickety bamboo bridge, and here the Anak Agung often took his siesta, alone or accompanied."

McPhee became a firm friend of Anak Agung Bagus and was a frequent guest at the palace: "... after we had eaten, I would walk through the park to the pavilion in the pond, which was given to me each time I came. Surrounded by water in this forgotten park, in this far island of friendly and mysterious people—this seemed the final exquisite isolation. In the stillness two turtle-doves called and answered monotonously. I read until I fell asleep."

The Taman Gili water garden at Klungkung contains the famous "floating pavilion" and the Kerta Gosa, also known as the "Hall of Justice," the only two buildings to survive the Dutch razing of the palace in 1908. The imposing, rectangular *bale kambang*, which appears to float above its lily-filled moat, is not, in fact, the original building, but an enlarged structure built in 1942. Every square inch of the panels beneath its ironwood shingled roof is covered with richly painted motifs in ink and natural pigments.

Balinese Temples and Shrines

There are literally tens of thousands of temples and shrines on the island of Bali, a proliferation of religious architecture probably not equalled anywhere else in the world. Behind the "exoticisim" and "mystery" of these sanctuaries is an underlying logic which determines the layout of the sanctuary and the symbolic significance of the individual structures in the temple precincts.

Glimpsed through a screen of trees, or across a swathe of verdant rice fields, the Balinese temple, set in its precinct, seems almost to be a part of the natural order of things. Closer to hand, the crumbling brickwork and lichen-covered statuary convey a sense of considerable antiquity, while the astonishing sculptural repertoire of demonic masks, multi-limbed deities, and lurid depictions of sexuality that confront the Western eye, conjure up an exotic otherness of "lost" civilizations and licentious natives—the "Mysterious East" of all good Orientalist fantasies. Throughout much of the year the temples lie eerily deserted, coming to life in a burst of activity on the date of their anniversary festival.

Balinese Religion

The religion of Bali represents an eclectic blend of Hindu and Buddhist beliefs laid over a much older stratum of indigenous animism, and it is this combination of native and exotic influences which informs so much of Balinese life. The introduction of Indian religious beliefs to Southeast Asia began about the time of Christ, and represents not so much a story of conquest and colonization as one of cultural assimilation which followed in the wake of burgeoning trade links with the subcontinent. In the case of Bali, bronze edicts, written in Old Balinese, testify to the existence of an Indian-style court by the end of the 9th century. However,

Temples and the Tripartite Division of the Universe

The Balinese division of the universe (*tri loka*) into three domains—*buhr*, *buwah*, and *swah*—corresponds to the concept of *tri angga*, which posits that everything in the Balinese cosmos can be similarly divided into three components: *nista*, *madya*, and *utama* (page 6). These categories are hierarchically ordered in terms of a set of spatial coordinates—high, middle, and low—which in the case of humans find a corporeal correspondence in a division of the body into three constituent parts—head, torso, and feet. Buildings and other man-made objects can similarly be divided into three components. A simple column, for example, consists of a base, a shaft, and a capital. This tripartite scheme of things ultimately extends to everything in the universe, from the Hindu trinity (*trimurti*) of Brahma, Siwa, and Wisnu, to the works of man, including the temples that he builds, reflecting an essential unity underlying the whole of creation.

ABOVE **A bell tower within the Pura Taman Ayun temple in Mengwi shows the traditional tripartite division in architectural terms.**

LEFT **The tripartite division of spaces inside a typical Balinese village temple is shown in the drawing at the left. The more "profane" spaces in the first courtyard on the seaward end (right side in this drawing), just inside the main entrance. Here are found the pavilions for the gamelan orchestras and the *kulkul* drum tower, used to communicate with the villagers. In the middle courtyard are the pavilions for storing ritual objects, for the preparation of offerings, and for use by priests. The third and most sacred courtyard on the left end (facing the mountains) is reserved for pavilions housing sacred ritual paraphernalia as well as shrines, pavilions and multi-tiered *meru* pagodas where the deities descend and are feted on festival days.**

Balinese Hinduism, as we know it today, owes more to influences from East Java between the 14th and 16th centuries. These Javanese influences have subsequently been shaped by local traditions to create a singular form of Hinduism peculiar to Bali.

Reincarnation and a Cosmic Order

Hinduism is founded on the assumption of a cosmic order which extends to every aspect of the universe, down to the very smallest particle. This organizing principle, or *dharma*, manifests itself in the persona of the gods, while demonic figures represent agents of disorder and chaos. As far as man is concerned, he must try to conduct himself in a manner which is in keeping with his own personal *dharma*, the ultimate aim here being to gain liberation (*moksa*) from the endless cycle of rebirth or reincarnation to which he is otherwise destined. This objective can only be achieved by establishing a harmonious relationship with the rest of the universe, a beatific state which requires the subjugation of all worldly desires.

The Balinese Lingga

Unlike their Indian counterparts, Balinese shrines and sanctuaries do not generally include a physical representation of the deity to whom they are dedicated. There are, however, exceptions, as in the case of Pura Penulisan, situated high on the crater walls surrounding Mt. Batur, where one finds this fine example of a stone *lingga*. In Hindu iconography, the *lingga* is a representation of the Hindu god Siwa, the phallic symbolism of the image being a celebration of the creative aspect of the deity. The veneration of Siwa plays an important role in Balinese religion, but *lingga* are found only in the oldest sanctuaries.

Microcosm and Macrocosm

Being in harmony with the rest of the universe requires that one be correctly oriented in space. These ideas are represented, on the ground so to speak, in terms of local topographical features and the cardinal directions, which are attributed specific ritual and cosmological significations. In this respect, the island of Bali is conceived as a replica of the universe in miniature—a microcosm of the macrocosm.

Central to this scheme of things is the idea of a tripartite universe consisting of an underworld (*buhr*), inhabited by demons and malevolent spirits; the world of men (*buwah*); and the heavens (*swah*), where the gods and deified ancestors reside. In Bali, the mountains are conceived as the holiest part of the island and thus the main places of worship are here. The sea is cast as a region of impurity and malign influences. Mankind is sandwiched in between, tending to his rice fields and visiting his temples to pay his obeisances to the gods and placate the forces of evil.

OPPOSITE ABOVE Shrines and pagodas inside a compound in the "Mother Temple" at Besakih, high on the flanks of Mt. Agung, Bali's highest volcano. Shrines from all around Bali are represented here and are always oriented so that people praying to them face the mountain's peak.

TOP Shrines within the Pura Dalem Jagaraga in northern Bali are oriented in the opposite direction to temple shrines in the south, since people praying to them must always face north toward the mountain.

ABOVE Entrance gates of Balinese temples are shaped like mountains.

The Archetypal Temple

Although no two Balinese temples are exactly alike, they conform to a basic pattern comprising walled courtyards separated by ornate gateways which is virtually the same all over the island. Things could not be otherwise, for Balinese temples are laid out according to strict cosmological principles, and to alter the basic design would be to admit to a change in the nature of the universe.

The idea of ritual purity plays a crucial role in Balinese religion, being identified as an essential requirement for a favorable reincarnation in the next life. Closely linked to the notion of a universal or cosmic order, it rests, in part, on the understanding that everything has its proper place in the world, and that one must be correctly positioned in relation to the rest of the universe if one is to achieve a state of grace according to the principles of *dharma*. Buildings are subject to the same rules of orientation and must be properly aligned if they are to serve the purpose they were designed for.

As we have seen, in Bali the mountains are the most holy of places, being identified as the abode of the gods, while the sea is represented as their antithesis, a place of impurity, the home of monstrous demons and other malevolent agencies. These ideas are defined locally by the terms *kaja* ("toward the mountains") and *kelod* ("toward the sea"), and in southern Bali, where the majority of the island's population live, they correspond roughly with a north-south axis (page 9).

East (*kangin*) and west (*kauh*) are also

Layout of a Temple

1 *Bale kulkul*, or drum tower.
2 *Bale gong*, a pavilion for gamelan performances.
3 *Gedong sinub westra*, a pavilion for storing ritual paraphernalia.
4 *Peranteng*, a kitchen for the preparation of food and offerings.
5 *Piasan pedanda*, a pavilion reserved for priests.
6 *Apit lawang*, paired shrines flanking the gateways leading into each of the courtyards, where offerings are placed for the guardians of the temple precincts.
7 *Pesantian*, a pavilion for performing ritual invocations.
8 *Piasan dauh*, a pavilion for storing ritual paraphernalia.
9 *Piasan ratu gede*, a pavilion for ritual paraphernalia.
10 *Pelinggih gedong*, a pavilion dedicated to the temple founder.
11 *Padmasana*, a shrine dedicated to the supreme godhead and prime mover of the universe, Ida Sanghyang Widhi Wasa.
12 *Pewedaan betara*, where the gods receive the prayer of the priests.
13 *Pewedaan pemangku*, a pavilion where lay priests offer prayers.
14 *Peselang*, a pavilion for holding small-scale rituals.

Mount Meru

The idea of mountains as holy places, as the abode of the gods, finds a natural accord with Indian mythology where the deities are portrayed as living in caves on the slopes of a sacred mountain—Mt. Meru or Mahameru—situated at the center of the universe. In Bali, this legendary mountain is generally identified with Gunung Agung, at 3014 m the highest peak on the island. Architecturally, Mt. Meru is represented by a tower-like edifice of the same name. The latter are wooden structures standing on a masonry base, surmounted by a series of stepped roofs, placed one on top of another, which give them a general appearance not unlike that of a Chinese pagoda. Interestingly, the idea of a sacred mountain would also seem to be part of a much older cultural tradition in the region: prehistoric stone terraces, cut into the sides of prominent peaks, have been found in many parts of the Indonesian archipelago, including Bali.

Pagodas on islets in the crater lake at Pura Ulun Danu Bratan.

important here: the east, where the sun rises, is identified with new life and other positive values, while the west, where it sets, is associated with death and decay. The point at which the sun reaches its zenith in the course of its daily passage makes up a third component in this scheme of things, which when combined with the *kaja-kelod* axis creates a ninefold division of space based on the four cardinal directions, their four intermediaries, and the center. This constitutes a kind of Balinese "compass rose," the *nawa-sanga*, where each point on the compass is identified with a particular deity in the Hindu pantheon and is ascribed a corresponding set of ritual or symbolic associations. In southern Bali, the northeast is conceived as the most auspicious, or sacred, direction, being a combination of "toward the mountains" and "east" (*kaja-kangin*).

Planning the Ideal Temple

The archetypal Balinese temple, or *pura*, consists of a series of three walled courtyards aligned on a linear axis running from the mountains to the sea. Ornamented gateways lead from one courtyard to the next, and as one crosses each threshold, one steps up a level.

In symbolic terms, the temple complex constitutes a spatial metaphor for the Hindu cosmos, the three courtyards replicating the tripartite nature of the universe, with each ascending level representing a higher state of purity or sacredness.

The outermost courtyard, or *jaba*, serves as a reception area where people gather at festivals to eat and socialize, while the middle courtyard, or *jaba tengah*, represents a transitional space between the secular world of men and the sacred domain of the gods. The latter is constituted by the innermost courtyard, or *jeroan*, which stands at the *kaja* end of the temple complex and is oriented toward the mountains from which, it is everyone's hope, that the gods will descend during temple ceremonies. This is where the most important shrines and ritual structures are located and where the gods are seated during temple festivals.

Other structures within the temple precincts include open-sided pavilions which provide protection for the priests when they are performing their ritual duties and constitute a work space when the community is preparing for a temple ceremony. One pavilion will be reserved as a place for the gamelan orchestra to perform.

A Resting Place for the Gods

Balinese temples are not conceived as places where the gods are permanently in residence, but rather as temporary sanctuaries where the gods alight when they descend from the heavens to attend a temple ceremony. During this time, the gods are invited to inhabit small wooden effigies, placed in the different kinds of shrines within the temple precincts, to which the villagers make offerings.

Unlike Hindu temples in India and in ancient Java, there are no physical representations of the deities housed in the various pavilions and shrines that provide a sanctuary for the gods during Balinese temple festivals. The gods are, however, invited to inhabit small wooden effigies called *pratima*. The latter come in pairs, the larger, more animal-like of the two representing the mount upon which the deity rides.

The most important ritual structures are situated in the inner sanctum, or *jero-an*, but there are places for offerings located at other strategic points in the temple complex, for example, on either side of the principal gateways which lead from one courtyard to another. The gateways play an important part in the symbolic order of Balinese temple architecture, creating thresholds between the secular world outside and the realm of the sacred within.

Padmasana: The "Lotus Seat"

There are two principal types of shrine, the *padmasana*, or "lotus seat," and the *meru*, a wooden house-like

LEFT **The *padmasana* is, in effect, a representation of the cosmos in miniature. The base is divided vertically into three stepped platforms corresponding to the three principle divisions of the cosmos: *buhr* (the netherworld of the demons), *buwah* (the realm of man), and *swah* (the domain of the gods). A stone throne sits on top with a high back, which is often ornamented with a carving of a swan or, alternatively, an eagle, the swan being identified as the mount, or vehicle, of Brahma, and the eagle that of Wisnu.**

OPPOSITE TOP **Three dramatic stairways lead up to white *kori agung* gates at Pura Penataran Agung Lempuyang temple high on the slopes of Mt. Seraya, in east Bali. From here you have gorgeous views of nearby Mt. Agung, Bali's highest volcano**

The Candi Bentar Split Gate

The *candi bentar*, or split gateway, is a distinctive feature of Balinese temple architecture. It typically stands at the main entrance to a temple or on the threshold of the outer and middle courtyards where it marks a transition from the secular world to the sacred domain of the inner precincts. In elevation, the *candi bentar* characteristically has a stepped profile, lavishly decorated with carvings and reliefs, though the two inner surfaces, as one passes through the portal, are left sheer and unornamented. The architectural origins of *candi bentar* date back to the days of the Majapahit empire in Java (1292–c.1525), though the symbolism of the gateway is uncertain.

structure with a masonry base and a multi-tiered roof. The *padmasana* is a small stone seat, raised about one and a half meters off the ground, and is intended as a resting place for the gods when they attend a temple festival. There are three basic types, classified according to the number of seats provided. The single-seater version is identified as the throne of Siwa, or alternatively, the sun god Surya. The double-seated version is dedicated to the deified ancestors, one male and one female. A triple-seated version may also be dedicated to the ancestors, or alternatively to the Hindu trinity (*trimurti*) of Brahma, Siwa, and Wisnu. The most important *padmasana* is placed in the most sacred (*kaja-kangin*) corner of the inner courtyard with its back to Mt. Agung. This shrine is dedicated to the Supreme Deity, Ida Sanghaya Widhi Wasa, in his manifestation as Siwa Raditya, the Balinese counterpart of Surya. The *padmasana* has recently become more prominent.

Meru: The Abode of the Gods

The *meru* symbolizes the legendary Mt. Meru of Indian mythology, which is identified as the abode of the gods. Individual *meru* will either be dedicated to specific gods

ABOVE **Close-up of a small shrine inside the village temple of Batuan. Shrines like these are designed as "mini** *meru*" **and are occupied by the gods during festival days. The painting on the shrine shows Sang Hyang Widi, the Balinese supreme being, and his consort.**

The Peppelik or Panuman

Located at the center of the inner sanctum, this serves as the communal seat of the gods when they descend from the heavens during a festival. There are also miniature houses for Ngrurah Alit and Ngrurah Gede, secretaries of the gods, who monitor the offerings, and a stone niche for the *Taksu*, or interpreter, who enters the body of mediums during trance sessions.

in the Balinese Hindu pantheon, or a deified ancestor, or else the deity of a particular location or geographical feature, such as a mountain or lake. *Meru* are constructed from wood and are raised on stilts, like miniature houses. They stand on a masonry base and are surmounted by a series of thatched roofs of diminishing size. The number of roofs is always odd and reflects the status of the deity to whom the shrine is dedicated, the most prestigious being accorded 11 tiers. *Meru* are regularly erected in honor of the deities associated with the island's two highest peaks, Gunung Agung and Gunung Batur.

OPPOSITE **The main shrine inside the ancient Pura Kehen temple in Bangli, central Bali. This temple was established in the 13th century on the southern flanks of a wooded hill as the royal temple for the kingdom of Bangli. The magnificent 11-tiered *meru* shrine stands inside the inner sanctum at the temple's highest level.**

Construction Rites for a Meru

During construction rites for a *meru*, miniature iron implements are buried beneath the shrine, together with small quantities of gold and silver, lotus flowers, crabs, prawns, and a roast chicken. Where the rafters of the uppermost roof meet, there is a vertical column with a cavity into which is placed a small bowl containing either nine precious stones or else nine *pripih*. The latter are thin plates of various metals which are inscribed with cabalistic words. Excavations in Java reveal similar ritual practices were employed in the construction of the great Hindu–Buddhist temples of Indonesia's classical era.

Village Temples

Balinese society is complex and multifarious, being divided by social hierarchies based on caste, occupation, and descent. Social divisions, somewhat similar to the Indian caste system, are, however, mediated by the village temple system and the cycle of festivals associated with them, which draw these diverse groups together as common participants in a shared ritual undertaking.

As we have seen (page 72), the Balinese village is referred to by the term *desa*, which describes both the settlement and its immediate environs as a physical entity, and at the same time refers to a religious community, made up of local householders and their families, who are responsible for maintaining the ritual purity and spiritual well-being of the village and its surrounding lands. The latter is achieved by observing the local customary laws (*desa adat*) and by participating in the cycle of religious ceremonies that take place at temples in the village.

The actual village itself, as a collection of residential compounds, is subdivided into distinctive neighborhoods, or wards (*banjar*), each of which has its own local temple (*pura pamaskan*). The *banjar* are usually referred to as "eastern," "western," and "central," but are sometimes named according to the dominant profession or caste (see page 14) of their residents. Thus can be found *banjar pande* where smiths live, and *banjar brahmana* where members of the Brahman caste predominate.

Every *banjar* has specific ritual duties to fulfill, not only in relation to its own neighborhood temple, but also to the main village temples (*pura desa*). *Banjar* members also act together in secular matters, such as the maintenance of roads and the policing of the neighborhood.

In the not so distant past, the life of the ordinary man, or commoner, was largely restricted to his village and its surrounding rice fields, while at a *supra*-village level there existed an upper crust of priests, noblemen, and princes organized into a ruling élite. These divisions are still in evidence today—though the plight of the common man is far less onerous—but the village temple system and its ritual cycle of festivals help in mediating these barriers.

Pura Desa: The Main Village Temple

Pura desa are ideally placed in an auspicious location at the center of the village—a position which is both toward the mountains (*kaja*) and to the east (*kangin*). A sacred banyan tree is usually planted beside the entrance, which often grows to enormous proportions, providing a shady center at the heart of the community. A pavilion (*wantilan*) for cockfights is also located nearby (page 78). The sacrificial shedding of blood (*caru*) plays a crucial role in

The Three Main Village Temples

Balinese villages, like Balinese temples, are typically arranged along a linear axis running between the mountains and the sea. Each village has three main places of worship, the *kahyangan tiga*, which service the religious needs of the community. This system of three village temples is said to have been initiated by Mpu Kuturan, the legendary Javanese priest who was responsible for a reformation of Balinese Hinduism in the 11th century. The *pura puseh*, or temple of origin, dedicated to the community founders, is situated at the uphill (*kaja*) end of the village, as befits the rarefied status of the village ancestors, while the cemetery and temple of the dead, *pura dalem*, are located at the downhill (*kelod*) end, usually a little outside the village, reflecting the ritual pollution of death. The principal village temple, the *pura desa*, which constitutes the ritual and social focal point of the community, is typically situated at the heart of the settlement—in the village square or on a prominent crossroads. The three temples are linked with the gods of the Hindu trinity: the *pura puseh* with Brahma the creator, the *pura desa* with Wisnu the preserver, and the *pura dalem* with Siwa the destroyer.

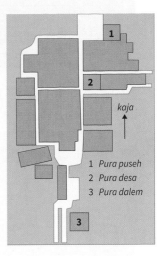

kaja

1 Pura puseh
2 Pura desa
3 Pura dalem

Balinese rituals, and contests are permitted on the occasion of a temple festival, though gambling is, in theory, illegal in Indonesia.

Village assemblies to discuss both ritual and secular matters are held every month, either at the *pura desa* itself or at the village assembly hall (*bale agung*), the "east" or "great pavilion," nearby and the secular counterpart of the *pura desa*. One of the principal responsibilities of the village assembly is the organization of the anniversary celebrations (*odalan*) for each of the village temples. The latter fall every 210 days, according to the sacred wuku calendar, and are intended to ritually cleanse the village territory and purify the members of the temple congregation. Various factors, such as local tradition and the size and importance of the ritual, determine whether a festival is officiated by the temple's own priest (*pemangku*) or by a Brahman high priest (*pedanda*).

Everyone in the village is involved in the preparation of offerings and the organization of various entertainments, such as gamelan recitals and shadow puppet performances, held for the enjoyment of the gods and mortals alike.

FAR LEFT **A *panuman* shrine inside the *pura desa* of Batuan, an important village for painters in Bali.**

CENTER LEFT **The main shrine in the innermost sanctum of Pura Griya Sakti Manuaba in Gianyar, dedicated to the 17th century founder of the temple, Pedanda Manuaba.**

BELOW **Women bear elaborate offerings of fruits and flowers to be placed in a village temple on its anniversary day. Dances, music, theatrical performance and rituals are performed on this day to entertain the gods who descend to enjoy the feast and the spectacles.**

Death and the Afterlife

Death in Bali is considered to be both ritually polluting and contaminating. These perceptions are reflected not only in the seaward (*kelod*) location of the community temple (*pura dalem*) where the funerary rites are held, and the nearby graveyard, but also in the Hindu deities associated with the *pura dalem* and the degradation of being interred underground rather than immediately cremated.

The *pura dalem* is located at the inauspicious, seaward end (*kelod*) of the village and also a little to the west, the setting sun in Bali being identified with the passing of life. The community graveyard and cremation site are located nearby. The cremation ground is usually simply a clearing in the cemetery at the most *kelod* end.

Pura dalem can often be spotted from some distance away by the presence of kapok (*Ceiba pentandra*) trees with their distinctive horizontal branches and cotton-bearing pods, which are frequently planted in the vicinity.

Siwa, Durga, and Rangda

Hindu deities are typically perceived as having a number of different attributes or guises, and *pura dalem* are usually dedicated to Siwa in his destructive aspect, though Siwa is, of course, also conceived as a god of creative energies. This apparent conflict of interests between these dual natures is not so much a case of contradiction as one of complementarity, for death, in the Hindu scheme of things, is merely one stage in an endless cycle of reincarnation, and in this last respect it is a necessary prelude to rebirth.

The creative aspect of Siwa is often personified in his wife Durga, but she, like her husband, has a dark, destructive side to her, metamorphosing into an incarnation of the goddess of death as the demonic, witch-like Rangda.

Death and the Fate of the Soul

Two explanations would seem to prevail in Balinese accounts of what happens to the soul after death. The first of these supposes that the correct performance of mortuary rituals, including cremation, ensures that the soul, which at the moment of death is impure, will subsequently be purified, thus enabling it to merge with a collective ancestral deity. The Balinese are rather vague about the precise nature of this aggregate ancestral spirit, but it is sometimes said to be responsible for the spiritual welfare and general health and well-being of living descendants.

The second point of view assumes that the soul of the deceased is subject to divine judgment based on the relative merit, or moral discredit, of deeds carried out during the dead person's lifetime. Depending on the final "score," which is reckoned according to the laws of *karma-pala* (literally, "actions" and their "fruit"), the soul is then sentenced to a period in the afterworld—either Heaven or Hell as the case may be—before being reborn into the world of the living again.

Burial and Cremation

Should the family of the deceased have sufficient funds, an immediate cremation is preferred since this skips the burial stage. In the case of members of a royal family, it is considered unseemly that such an illustrious corpse should be placed in the ground, so the body is preserved, lying in state in a special pavilion in the palace compound, until suitable preparations for a lavish cremation ceremony have been completed, and there is an auspicious day in the Balinese calendar for the ceremony to take place. The lying-in-state period may last for months, even years. (Priests are not buried either, there being a ritual prohibition on their interment.) After a day has been set, vast quantities of valuable ritual objects and offerings are specially created to accompany the burning corpse, which has been placed high up on a decorated tower.

Cremation (*ngaben*) releases the soul from its ties to the earth, returning the five elemental constituents of the body—earth, fire, water, air, and space—to the cosmos. The ashes are thrown in a river or cast upon the sea, with the final mortuary rites being held some twelve days later (longer for *triwangsa* castes). These complete the Balinese cycle of death rituals, at which point the newly purified soul becomes incorporated with those of the ancestors.

OPPOSITE FAR LEFT A statue of Rangda from the *pura dalem* at Gunung Salak, Tabanan. This demonic, witch-like creature with her tangled hair, lolling tongue and pendulous breasts, is identified as an agent of death and destruction. The word *rangda* in high Balinese means "widow."

LEFT An elaborate cremation tower in the shape of a winged temple decorated with benevolent spirits and flowers. The remains of the deceased are placed in the tower. Then it is brought to the cemetery to be burned in a spectacular display of pageantry.

ABOVE Remains of the deceased may also be placed inside black paper maché bulls to be cremated. Since cremations in Bali normally occur months or even years after someone's death, it is common for a number of families to pool their resources and hold the cremations of several people together, so they can share the expenses.

A Balinese Hades

Those who have led a less than meritorious life must face divine retribution in the next. The Balinese Hell (*Neraka*) is located in the subterranean world (*buhr*) of demons and malevolent spirits, and it is to this frightful place that the souls of the wicked are consigned after their demise. Their punishment depends on the kinds of misdemeanor they have committed during their lifetime. The post-mortem fate of those found guilty of evil misdoings are graphically portrayed in the temple reliefs at the *pura dalem*. The consequences of fornication and sexual misconduct are often an excuse to introduce an erotic or ribald element into these images, which can be a source of amusement and titillation for both Balinese and tourists.

Sacred Rice and Subak Temples

Rice and its cultivation are central to the Balinese way of life. In Balinese eyes, rice is a gift from the gods. It was created by the Hindu deity Wisnu who then presented it to man as his divine patrimony. Rice is thus a sacred thing whose cultivation entails not only planting and nurturing the crop, but also the careful implementation of a set of ritual processes first laid down by the god Indra.

The modern Balinese farmer grows two crops of rice each year in irrigated, terraced rice fields which for many are the definitive feature of the Balinese landscape. Water sources in the mountains are directed to each individual rice field by an intricate network of channels and aqueducts, whose maintenance and regulation are governed by local cooperative organizations called *subak*. Each mini-watershed has its own *subak* council, made up from neighboring farmers who are party to this supply and who are responsible for the equable distribution of water to all the irrigated rice fields within their purview.

Each *subak* council has its own temple (*ulun carik*), situated in the middle of the rice fields, belonging to its members, and this is where the major ceremonies of the rice cycle are held. The temple of Ulun Danu, on the shores of Lake Bratan, is identified as the "mother" temple of all the *subak* systems on the island and some associations make regular pilgrimages here prior to irrigating their rice fields. There are also countless small, roofless shrines (*bedugul*), which are commonly found in cultivated areas, typically beside a dam or weir, but often in the middle of a rice field. These tend to be erected and maintained by individual farmers whose fields are in the vicinity.

LEFT **The goddess of rice is honored with offerings in a simple ceremony in the middle of the rice fields.**

Dewi Sri

Rice has been cultivated in Asia for several thousands of years and everywhere that it is grown it is surrounded by ritual prescriptions and prohibitions. Rice is commonly assumed to have a soul, whose presence, or absence, determines the success, or failure, of the harvest. Often the increase of rice is symbolically identified with the fertility of women; in Bali, the ripening rice plants are said to be "pregnant" (*beling*) while the principal rice deity is the goddess Dewi Sri, who is the perfect realization of feminine grace and charm.

Pura Ulun Danu Bratan

Built by the ruler of Mengwi in 1633, Pura Ulun Danu Bratan—the temple of the lake goddess—is much revered as a source of fertility. It consists of four compounds, two of which are detached from the main temple complex on little islets a few meters from the shore of Lake Bratan. A bubbling spring, together with a large white stone flanked by two red ones—a phallic *lingga* no less—were uncovered during restoration of the three-tiered *meru* on one of the islets, indicating a Sivaite connection. The main *meru* with the 11-tiered roof on the neighboring islet is dedicated to Wisnu in his manifestation as the lake goddess Dewi Danu, the savior of all living creatures. As well as being the creator of rice and the husband of the rice goddess Dewi Sri, Wisnu is also responsible for regulating the flow of terrestrial waters, hence his association with *subak* temples.

A Balinese Harvest Home

The most important *subak* ceremony in the Balinese agricultural cycle is the festival of *ngusaba nini*, which is usually held either just before or immediately after the rice harvest. It is held at the *subak* association temple and takes the form of a thanksgiving ceremony dedicated to the rice goddess Dewi Sri. Dewi Sri is the wife of Wisnu and is one of the most popular deities in the Balinese pantheon, being conceived as the paragon of everything that is good and beautiful. Furthermore, as rice goddesss, she is identified as the fountainhead of agricultural fertility and bountiful harvests, while her daughter, Dewi Melanting, is considered the tutelary deity of seed and plants.

For the rites of *ngusaba nini*, a mouthwatering selection of offerings are prepared by members of the *subak* association. After they have been dedicated by the priests to the beneficent gods, and in particular to Dewi Sri, they are shared amongst the participants at the festival. As with all temple offerings, the gods are said to enjoy the essence (*sari*) of whatever is presented to them, leaving its material residue for the delectation of their followers.

BELOW **Pura Ulun Danu Tamblingan, the "Temple at the Source of Lake Tamblingan."** Several large lakes sit inside the craters of the volcanoes forming the central spine of Bali—including Bratan, Batur, Buyan and Tamblingan. These lakes are very deep and serve as year-round water reservoirs for the island, supplying water to springs on the flanks of the volcanoes. Each lake has an important temple where the Balinese go to give thanks to the gods for this life-giving water.

Sacred Bathing Places

Water has a special place in Balinese life, not only because of the vital role it plays in irrigating the island's rice fields, but also because of its ritual significance as an agent of purification and for its magical and curative properties. With its source in the volcanic lakes and rushing streams of the central mountain range, water is identified with the purity of gods who dwell on high.

As water flows from the mountains and lakes of the central range (the *kaja* part of the island) to the sea (the *kelod* part), where it enters the realm of greatest impurity, it picks up the dirt of man along the way, both in the literal sense—the Balinese are very conscious of personal cleanliness and bathe themselves in running water several times a day—and also in terms of spiritual pollution. It is in this last respect that water acts as a purifying agent, cleansing man of his mortal sins and preparing his soul for a better reincarnation in the next life.

Holy Water

Holy water (*tirtha*) is the principal means by which various forms of impurity are ritually washed down to the sea. The preparation of holy water is a sacrament of great importance in Balinese religion, which the Balinese often refer to as the *agama tirtha*, or "holy water religion." The degree of potency of holy water is contingent on its source, the status of the person who prepares it, and the type of mantra employed in its preparation. The holiest of holy waters comes from high up in the mountains.

ABOVE Telaga Waja, on the Tukad Kungkang River, consists of two pools, one is slightly higher than the other, filled by a spring located above the river. Three niches are cut into the hillside next to the upper pool and there is a small temple courtyard on a raised terrace to the south of the lower one, which is also surrounded by niches. The latter were probably used as places of meditation.

Sacred Bathing Places

Every village has a recognized bathing place—either the nearby river or a community bath, with separate compartments for men and women to perform their ablutions. In addition, there are numerous sacred pools and bathing places whose waters are deemed to have magical or curative qualities.

The central Balinese regency of Gianyar is particularly well-endowed with sacred bathing sites. The best known of these are Tirtha Empul, Pura Mengening, Telaga Waja, and Goa Gajah, but there are several other sacred bathing places in the vicinity of the Petanu and

Pakerisan rivers, which flow through Gianyar. Tirtha Empul is typical of most sacred bathing places in having a number of adjacent, rectangular pools surrounded by low walls into which clear, transparent water is directed through carved spouts ranged along the walls of the pools. Pavilions for the gods and numerous small shrines with decorated doors are also a feature of such sites.

In the Amlapura area, the water palace at Tirta Gangga, which literally means "Ganges Water" and refers to the sacred river of the Hindus, contains a series of formal pools fed by a sacred spring. Swimming is permitted in several designated pools.

ABOVE **The Pura Gunung Kawi Sebatu complex in Gianyar, north of Ubud, includes a large temple, a holy spring, pools and public bathing areas for men and women.**

LEFT **The ancient sacred spring and bathing pools of Pura Tirta Empul at Tampaksiring. This temple was founded in the 10th century and is one of the oldest in Bali. It is located at the source of the Pakerisan River which runs through the center of Gianyar Regency.**

LEFT One of the spring-fed pools at Pura Gunung Kawi Sebatu temple, previously used for bathing, but now filled with ornamental koi fish.

BELOW One of several bathing areas at Pura Tirta Empul, one of Bali's oldest temples, established more than a thousand years ago.

Tirtha Empul

The baths at Tirtha Empul are the most ancient and holy of Bali's sacred bathing places. A stone inscription at the nearby temple of Pura Sakenan, in the village of Manukaya, records that they were built by one Sang ratu (Sri) Candra Bhaya Singha Varmadeva, in the district of the village of Manuk Raya in the year 882 (around AD 960) according to the *saka* era calendar. Local legend, however, provides a more romantic account of their origin, attributing the baths to the god Indra who summoned forth the

spring which feeds them during a military campaign to overthrow the evil and despotic Balinese prince, Mayadenawa. One night, when Indra's troops were sleeping, Mayadenawa crept into their camp, and using his occult powers conjured up a poison spring. When Indra's men awoke and drank from the contaminated water, they became violently ill. Fortunately, Indra realized what had happened and immediately created a new spring from which gushed forth holy water, restoring his army to health.

ABOVE The reconstructed pools at the Tirtha Gangga (the name refers to the sacred River Ganges in India) water garden in eastern Bali, where water from a sacred spring is channeled through a number of fountains and water spouts. This water spout is carved from volcanic stone in the fanciful shape of a sacred cow. This pool was originally built in 1946 for the use of the royal family of Karangasem (now Amlapura).

BELOW One of the ancient water spouts at Tirtha Empul. Offerings of delicately-cut palm leaves with flowers and rice are placed on the water spouts by villagers on a daily basis to give thanks to the goddess of the spring.

Pura Besakih: Bali's "Mother Temple"

Mountains occupy a special place in Balinese cosmology, and there is none more sacred than Gunung Agung (Mt. Agung), the island's highest peak, which is regarded as the navel of the world. Local legend has it that it is actually the summit of Mt. Meru brought from India by the god Paramasiwa when Hinduism was introduced to the island. It is the home of the mother temple for all Bali, Pura Besakih.

Pura Besakih, which is situated on the southern slopes of Gunung Agung at an altitude of 900 meters, was at one time the principal place of worship for the royal families of Klungkung, Karangasem, and Bangli, but today is regarded as the mother temple for the whole of the island of Bali. It is indisputably the most important temple complex on the island. Although Pura Besakih has very ancient origins, the present structures are of comparatively recent construction, with few dating back to before the earthquake of 1917. Nevertheless, despite the many renovations that have taken place over the centuries, Pura Besakih still retains its archaic character—some suppose that it may stand on the site of a prehistoric place of worship belonging to the island's pre-Hindu-Buddhist past.

The 1963 Eruption of Mt. Agung

In 1963, Gunung Agung blew its top in the middle of the month-long celebrations of Eka Dasda Rudra. Although the eruption caused great destruction in the vicinity, the lava flow came to a halt just before it engulfed the Pura Besakih. The eruption was interpreted as the wrath of the gods, who were said to be displeased either by the timing of the festival (this was a period of extreme political tensions) or else with the manner in which the rites were conducted. In 1979, the ceremony was held more favorably in the presence of President Suharto.

Three Lotus Thrones

The symbolic center of the Pura Besakih complex are the lotus thrones, or *padmasana*, in the main Pura Penataran Agung sanctuary, which dates to the 17th or 18th century. Visited by tens of thousands of Balinese during major festivals, this focus of prayer and worship takes the form of a three-seated throne dedicated to the godhead Ida Sanghyang Widhi Wasa, as manifested in the triple persona of Siwa, Sadasiwa, and Paramasiwa or, alternatively, the Hindu triumvirate of Brahma, Siwa, and Wisnu. The view here shows the three *padmasana* elaborately adorned with fabrics and woven palm-leaf banners on a festival day.

The Pura Besakih Complex

The complex comprises 22 temples situated on parallel ridges running down the mountainside of Gunung Agung, producing a panorama of hundreds of delicately towering *meru*. The main temple is Pura Penataran Agung, or the "Great State Temple," dedicated to the god Siwa, who occupies the most prominent position in the Balinese pantheon. Pura Batu Madeg, or the "Temple of the Erect Stone"—a reference to the phallic-shaped monolith that it houses—stands a little to the left (as one faces toward Gunung Agung) and is dedicated to Brahma, the creator. Pura Dangin Kreteg, or "Temple East of the Bridge," is situated on the other side of the main sanctuary, over a bridge and across a gully, and is dedicated to Wisnu. Together the three deities constitute the Hindu triumvirate, or *trimurti*. Another 19 temples spread up the mountain slopes, a great many of which are dedicated to other Balinese gods. Several ancestral temples on the site venerate the deified ances-

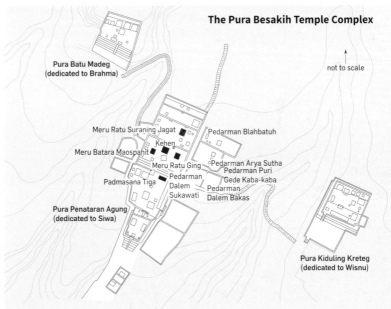

The Pura Besakih Temple Complex

Pura Batu Madeg
(dedicated to Brahma)

not to scale

Meru Ratu Suraning Jagat
Kehen
Meru Batara Maospahit
Meru Ratu Ging
Pedarman
Padmasana Tiga
Dalem
Sukawati
Pura Penataran Agung
(dedicated to Siwa)

Pedarman Blahbatuh

Pedarman Arya Sutha
Pedarman Puri
Gede Kaba-kaba
Pedarman
Dalem Bakas

Pura Kiduling Kreteg
(dedicated to Wisnu)

TOP The "stairway to heaven" leading up to Pura Penataran Agung, the main temple at Besakih.

tors of various clans, including the royal houses of Klung-kung, Karangasem, and Bangli.

Pura Penataran Agung

Pura Penataran Agung is the symbolic center of the Besakih complex and comprises six terraces which bear witness to successive enlargements, the most recent being in 1962. There are 57 structures in the temple sanctuary dedicated to various members of the Balinese pantheon, the principal deity being Siwa. The *meru* towers were probably introduced during the 14th century, possibly in response to Majapahit influences. The lotus throne, or *padmasana*, dates from the 17th or 18th century and acts as the ritual focus of the *pura*, and indeed the Besakih complex as a whole.

The Annual Cycle of Festivals

More than 70 festivals are held regularly at Pura Besakih with almost every shrine in the temple complex celebrating its own anniversary each year. These festive cycles are generally tied to the 210-day *wuku* calendrical system, but the most important ceremonies follow the lunar calendar. The great annual festival of Bhatara Turun Kabeh (literally, "The Gods Descend Together") lasts for a whole month and takes place during the tenth lunar month of the year, somewhere between March or April. At this time, it is supposed that the gods of all the temples in Bali, great and small, take up residence in the main sanctuary at Pura Besakih, and tens of thousands of people from all over the island come to worship at the *padmasana*.

Ritual Purification of the Universe

Pura Besakih is also the site of the greatest Balinese ceremony of all, the Eka Dasda Rudra, or Purification of the Universe, which is held once every hundred years—when the *saka* year of the Balinese calendar ends with two zeros. It draws almost everyone on the island. The principal aim is to placate and propitiate Rudra, one

of the most ancient of Indian deities, pre-Hindu in his origin, who is associated with disease, plagues, tempestuous winds, and other natural disasters.

TOP **A group of villagers brings the idols from their village temple to pay a visit to the main shrine at Pura Besakih. Yellow umbrellas, a sign of royalty, are held above the idols to signify their divinity.**

ABOVE **One of more than 70 festivals held in the main courtyard of Pura Penataran Agung each year, in which hundreds of participants bring offerings to pray and be sprinkled with holy water.**

Pura Luhur Uluwatu

The spectacularly located Pura Luhur Uluwatu, on the westernmost tip of the rocky Bukit Peninsula, is one of the *sad kahyangan*, or "six great sanctuaries," on the island of Bali. The temple is dedicated to the supreme godhead, Ida Sanghyang Widhi Wasa, in his manifestation of Rudra, the dissolver of life, who can conjure up violent storms, volcanic eruptions, and other cataclysmic interventions of nature.

Both the inner and outer gateways of Pura Luhur Uluwatu are flanked by statues of the elephant god Ganesha, which is quite unusual in Bali. Ganesha is identified as the remover of obstacles, especially in literary and educational matters. In this last respect, he has come to be identified with the acquisition of wisdom.

Pura Uluwatu is also associated with the legendary Nirartha, who is credited with being the principal architect of a 16th-century Hindu Renaissance in Bali around the time of the collapse of the Majapahit dynasty in East Java (pages 30–31). Like Mpu Kuturan, Nirartha founded many temples and encouraged the building of *padmasana* shrines at existing sanctuaries, including the *padmasana* at Pura Uluwatu. It is claimed that it was at Pura Uluwatu that Nirartha achieved his final liberation from the endless cycle of rebirth, becoming one with the godhead. This singular event resulted in the word *luhur* being added to the name of the temple; *luhur* comes from the verb *ngeluhur*, meaning "to go up," a reference to the apotheosis of Nirartha.

The Temple

Pura Uluwatu is built from dark gray coral stone, which is much harder and more durable than the volcanic tuff which is normally used for most Balinese temples. This has meant that the stone sculptures and decorative elements are better preserved here than in the case of

ABOVE **Both the inner and outer gateways of Pura Uluwatu are flanked by statues of the elephant god Ganesha, which is quite unusual in Bali. Ganesha is identified as the remover of obstacles, especially in literary and educational matters. In this last respect, he has come to be identified with the acquisition of wisdom.**

RIGHT **Pura Luhur Uluwatu perches on a vertical cliff 70 meters (225 feet) above the Indian Ocean at the southwesternmost tip of Bali. It is one of the most dramatic spots on the island and a temple has existed here at least since the 11th century. This is where the priest Nirartha is said to achieved *moksa* (release from earthly cares) and ascended to the heavens to become one with the Supreme Being, Sang Hyang Widhi Wasa.**

Kori Agung

The middle courtyard of Pura Luhur Uluwatu is dominated by a *kori agung* gateway which leads into the inner sanctum. Its design is very unusual for Bali, being distinguished by an arch, or *gapura*, an architectural device which seldom occurs in the Balinese repertoire. The arch has no keystone as such, the apex being completed instead by two large horizontal blocks which perform the function of a lintel. Over the top of the arch there is a leering Bhoma head to deter malign influences from entering the inner sanctum. Above this stands a sculpture of the *kamandalu,* the sacred vessel which holds the elixir of life.

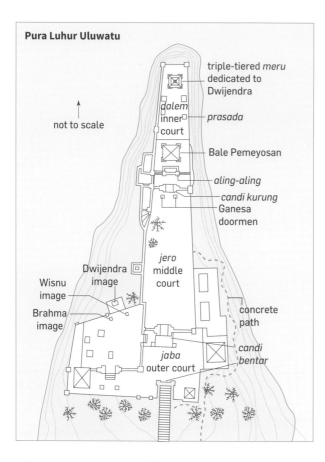

Pura Luhur Uluwatu

not to scale

triple-tiered *meru* dedicated to Dwijendra

dalem inner court

prasada

Bale Pemeyosan

aling-aling

candi kurung
Ganesa doormen

jero middle court

Dwijendra image

Wisnu image

Brahma image

concrete path

candi bentar

jaba outer court

kori agung gateway leading into the inner sanctum is quintessentially Balinese, namely the head of Bhoma. Some of these are surmounted by an image of Mt. Meru, the cosmic mountain at the center of the Hindu-Buddhist universe, while over the *kori agung* gateway one finds a representation of an urn. The latter is identified as the sacred vessel holding ambrosia (*amrt*a), the immortal elixir of life, which in Indian mythology was extracted by the gods from the primeval ocean of milk.

Lightning Strikes

Only those who have come to pray may enter the inner

other ancient sites. It is difficult, however, to put a precise date to the existing structures because the temple has been renovated and rebuilt many times during the course of its long history. At the very beginning of this century, part of the temple collapsed into the sea, which required substantial reparations, while the most recent restoration work was carried out in the 1980s.

The projecting limestone rock on which the temple of Uluwatu stands, 250 meters above the Indian Ocean, is said to be the petrified bark of Dewi Danu, goddess of the waters.

The three *candi bentar* gateways at Pura Uluwatu are unusual in that the upper portions have been sculpted in the shape of wings—the Balinese themselves refer to this type of *candi bentar* as "winged" (*bersayap*). The oldest of the three *candi bentar*, which leads into the central courtyard, is also incised with stylized flying birds thought to be a Balinese version of the Chinese phoenix. Exotic influences notwithstanding, the principal motif ornamenting all three *candi bentar* and the sanctum, but one can get a general view from a terrace on the southern side of the central courtyard. The most important structure in the enclosure is a three-tiered *meru* which stands at the far end. This was struck by lightning a few years back, a very singular and inauspicious event, which could only be redressed by elaborate rites of purification and a rededication of the temple.

BELOW AND RIGHT An amphitheater has been created just next to Pura Luhur Uluwatu and tourist performances of the dramatic Kecak dance are performed here every day at sunset. This is undoubtedly one of the most dramatic spectacles found anywhere in Bali.

The Balinese Village

The Balinese village, or *desa*, denotes both the settlement and its immediate physical environs (*tanah desa*), as well as a religious community made up of local householders and their families who are responsible for maintaining the ritual purity and spiritual well-being of the *tanah desa*. This they do by observing local customary laws (*desa adat*) and by participating in religious ceremonies.

The typical Balinese village is laid out on a *kaja-kelod* axis running between the mountains and the sea (page 7), often in defiance of local topographical considerations.

The approach is signalled by a *candi bentar* (split gateway), with the road typically executing a sharp S-bend a little after this. Like the *aling-aling* "blind" wall immediately inside the entrance to the compound, the S-bend strategy outside it is another tactic intended to prevent malevolent spirits from entering the village—the spirits are said to have difficulty negotiating sharp corners.

The center of the community is usually defined by a crossroads and a large square, or *bancingah*, which is kept free of built structures but often has a huge banyan tree at one end to provide shade. The main village temple (*pura desa*) is usually located in the most propitious corner (*kaja-kangin*) of this open space, although the site may alternatively be occupied by the palace (*puri*) of a local prince.

Other important public buildings associated with the center of the village include the local assembly hall (*bale agung*) and a drum tower (*bale kulkul*), which is used to summon the community to meetings and to warn of danger.

Penglipuran Village north of Bangli, in central-eastern Bali, has turned itself into a handicraft and homestay center for tourists. Here you can experience traditional village life in a house compound.

Layout of a Typical Balinese Village

1 *Pura puseh*
2 *Pura desa*
3 *Bancingah*
4 *Wantilan*
5 *Pura dalem and graveyard*

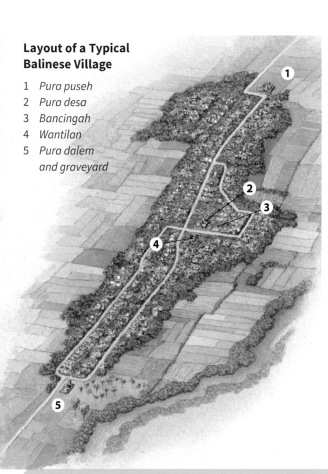

ABOVE AND LEFT Balinese towns and villages are aligned on a north-south axis running from the mountains down to the sea (the same direction as streams and rivers). Uphill areas are regarded as closer to heaven and therefore more sacred whereas downhill areas are more polluted. The locations of temples and meeting pavilions within the village always follow the pattern shown in the drawing on the left.

LEFT Any village or settlement of reasonable size will consist of a number of smaller residential groupings or neighborhoods, called *banjar*, each with their own local temple or *pura pamaskan*. Family compounds, belonging to the same *banjar*, tend to be laid out in rows on either side of a street or lane, and these rows of adjacent compounds, which are called *tempek*, often act together in performing the various communal duties or obligations. Each *banjar* has specific ritual duties to fulfill, not only in relation to its own neighborhood temple, but also to the main village temples. *Banjar* members also act together in secular matters such as the maintenance of roads and the policing of the neighborhood.

Village Assemblies

Village assemblies (*sangkepan desa*), attended by family heads, are held every month at the *pura puseh* or at the assembly hall (*bale agung*) nearby, during which matters of both ritual and secular importance are addressed. One of their principal responsibilities is to organize the anniversary celebrations (*odalan*) of each of the village temples. These "birthday" festivals, which fall every 210 days according to the Balinese ceremonial *wuku* calendar, are extremely important to the life of the community, being intended to ritually cleanse the village territory (*tanah desa*) and purify all the members of the temple congregation. Everyone in the local community is drawn into the preparation of offerings and organizing the various entertainments. These include gamelan recitals, shadow puppet theater, human dance-dramas, masked dances and operetta for the enjoyment of both gods and mortals.

Each person in Bali is expected to participate in regular village-wide temple and anniversary celebrations, even if they live and work elsewhere on the island. Since there are three temples in each village and the anniversary celebrations are held at each temple every 210 days, plus the island-wide New Year's celebrations (also held every 210 days), this means there is a major festival somewhere in Bali almost every day!

ABOVE **A typical village street with walled house compounds on either side. All of the streets and houses are aligned on a north-south axis running from the sea up to the mountains.**

LEFT **Village temple celebrations are a chance for the entire village to assemble and play music, watch dance and theater performances, or just talk to their friends and have a good time.**

There may also be a special pavilion for holding cockfights, a favorite Balinese pastime. This is called a *wantilan* and is often quite an impressive structure with a soaring roof and elegant columns.

Kahyangan Tiga

Balinese villages should ideally have at least three core temples, which between them serve the religious needs of the community and are the sites for the cycle of religious ceremonies that take place in the village.

In addition to the main village temple, which is situated at the center of the village, there is also a temple honoring the founding fathers of the community and

another dedicated to the dead. Their respective locations, in relation to the center of the village, can be understood in the context of Balinese ideas of ritual sanctity and pollution: the ancestral temple, or "temple of origin" (*pura puseh*) is placed at the *kaja* end of the village as befits the deified status of the community founders, while the temple for the not-yet-purified deceased (and of magically charged and potentially dangerous forces), the *pura dalem*, is located at the *kelod* end, reflecting the polluting nature of death. By the same reasoning, the community graveyard and cremation ground too are, typically, situated nearby.

The practice of having three village temples is said to have been begun by Mpu Kuturan, the revered Javanese priest, sage, and temple architect who was responsible for a reformation of Balinese Hinduism during the 11th century, at a time when the religion was in decline. The three temples are known collectively as the *kahyangan tiga* and they are identified with the Hindu trinity of Brahma, Wisnu, and Siwa.

ABOVE **A small Hindu shrine with elaborate carvings of dark-grey coral stone in Pemuteran, on the north coast of West Bali.**

BELOW **A procession of offerings and idols brought by villagers to a nearby temple for purposes of purification, in this case on the occasion of a full moon.**

Public Buildings

Every Balinese village has a number of public buildings or spaces where people come together at festivals and on other important social occasions to honor the gods, to discuss village affairs, or simply to meet. These include the three principal village temples that make up the *kahyangan tiga* system, an assembly hall (*bale agung*), the village square and marketplace, and a cockfighting pavilion (*wantilan*).

The threshold of the Balinese village is usually marked by a *candi bentar*, a split gateway. The *candi bentar*, which is a distinctive feature of Balinese architecture, is also used for temple entrances where it marks a transition from the secular world to the realm of the sacred.

In elevation, the *candi bentar* has a characteristic stepped or pyramid-shaped profile, which is lavishly decorated with carvings and reliefs. The carving is normally mirrored on either side. The two inner surfaces, as one passes through the gateway, are left sheer and unornamented to emphasize the division of the two sides.

The architectural origins of *candi bentar* can be traced to ancient Java and, in particular, to the East Javanese kingdom of Majapahit (late 13th–early 16th centuries), which was the last of the great Hindu-Buddhist empires in Indonesia's classical past. Ruins in the vicinity of Trowulan, which archeologists have identified as the former capital of Majapahit, include a massive example of a *candi bentar*, which may have been the ceremonial entrance to the city.

The symbolic significance of this bifurcated gateway remains unclear, but the Mexican artist and writer Miguel Covarrubias, who lived in Bali during the 1930s, records a pleasing Balinese account. He writes that the *candi bentar* represents the legendary Mt. Meru of Hindu mythology, which was split in two by Pasupati (Siwa) and placed in Bali as the twin peaks of Mt. Agung and Mt. Batur.

ABOVE **The *kulkul* drum tower in Penglipuran Village near Bangli.**

ABOVE LEFT **The center of a Balinese village is often presided over by a *rakshasa* statue, the village guardian. Similar statues guard the entrances to temples and palaces.**

LEFT **The huge split gate or *candi bentar* at the entrance to the Pura Puseh in the village of Batuan, on the road to Ubud.**

Bale Kulkul

The *bale kulkul* is a tower-like structure occupying a prominent position in the village. The *kulkul* itself is a percussive device consisting of a hollow piece of timber with a slit in one side. It resonates when struck, and is beaten to summon the local community to assemble. Different rhythms indicate the particular reason for the summons, for example, a meeting of household heads at the *bale agung*, or, in the past, a call to arms. The building in which the *kulkul* device is housed—where it is usually suspended from the rafters of the roof—may be simple or elaborate, depending on the wealth of the community.

ABOVE **A simple *bale kulkul* in the mountain village of Sutei.**

The elaborate *bale kulkul* in Banjar Abiankapas, Denpasar.

The Wantilan Cockfighting Pavilion

The cockfighting pavilion is a large and often quite imposing two- or three-tiered structure with a lofty, tiled roof raised on twelve coconut wood columns. It is typically found at the center of the Balinese village.

Cockfighting (*tajen*) once played a central role in the social life of the Balinese village, or at least in the lives of its menfolk, for women were prohibited from participating. Today, cockfighting is strictly regulated by the government, for all forms of gambling are illegal in the Republic of Indonesia, including betting on fighting cocks. However, cockfighting has very deep and ancient roots in Balinese culture, and is an important part of the male psyche. Because it involves the spilling of blood, it also has a ritual aspect to it, being seen as a propitiation to malevolent spirit influences (*bhuta* or *kala*). Consequently, the Indonesian government does allow a limited number of cockfights to be held in Bali on ceremonial occasions provided no betting takes place. Needless to say, this last stricture is rarely adhered to. Cockfights are still regularly held almost everywhere on the island, albeit discreetly, out of sight of the authorities.

TOP AND RIGHT **Cockfighting is still a popular pastime in Bali, despite the fact that gambling is officially banned. Sharp blades are attached to the heel of each cock and they battle until one dies. Onlookers bet on which one will win.**

One of the distinguishing features of the cockfighting pavilion (*wantilan*) is its pyramid-shaped roof, a characteristic it shares with shrines and other religious structures. The reason for this is that the *wantilan* is perceived as a sacred building; the shedding of blood during the cockfight is akin to offering a blood sacrifice to malevolent forces. This *wantilan* is at Banjar Tangkas, Kendran, in the south of Bali.

The Balinese House Compound

The initial stage of construction, when the overall dimensions of the compound are marked out and the plan of the different structures—and their relative position to one another—are laid out on the ground, is critical for determining both the character of the buildings erected and the potential fate of those who will occupy them.

As noted earlier, measurement and orientation play a crucial role in Balinese architecture. The first set of dimensions that must be determined, once the site of the compound has been selected, is its length and width overall. The basic unit of measurement employed here is the distance between the fingertips of the two hands when the arms are fully outstretched on either side of the body (*depa*). The sum of the lengths of two sides must add up to an odd number of these units, and their difference in length, when one is subtracted from the other, should also be an odd number of units. If there is a mistake in the measurements and their sum or difference happens to be an even number of units, it is said that the compound is "without doors," "closed" or "blocked." It is also said to be "like a body without a soul," in other words "dead" (*mati*). The explanation given is that a compound without doors provides no access for the gods and at the same time prevents the expulsion of malevolent influences. Such a site cannot support life, hence its designation as moribund.

Site Rituals

The various stages of construction and the eventual occupancy date are determined by auspicious dates in the Balinese calendar. Construction is inaugurated by the rite of *suci daksina peras ajuman panyeneng*, which is intended to purify the site. This rite involves placing supplicatory offerings at the "mountain" (*kaja*) end of the compound. A similar offering is also placed at the *kelod* end to placate malevolent spirits and other harmful agencies (*buta kala*). Each subsequent stage of construction must be accompanied by further offerings to negate malign influences.

Layout of the Compound

The first part of the building to be constructed after the

Grid Layout of the Compound

Conceptually, the Balinese residential compound can be divided in accordance with the *nawa-sanga* scheme of things into nine squares consisting of the eight cardinal directions and the center. The family shrines are positioned in the most auspicious corner of the compound, "toward the mountains" (*kaja*) and "toward the wind" (*kangin*). The sleeping pavilion (*meten*) of the head of the household, which is the next most important building in the compound, is positioned immediately to the west of the family temple, which reflects not only the senior position of the family head but also his relative proximity to the ancestors in terms of descent.

Kaja Kauh	Kaja	Kaja Kangin
Kauh	Puseh	Kangin
Kelod Kauh	Kelod	Kelod Kangin

inaugural rites have been conducted by the local priest are the walls of the compound. Once these are completed, temporary shrines are erected in the place where the family temple will eventually be built.

Work then starts on laying out the rest of the compound in accordance with the spatial precepts of the Balinese compass rose, or *nawa-sanga* (page 8), which provides a framework for the proper orientation of build-

Deities and Dimensions

Units of Measurement	Deity	Status or Attribute	Compass Direction
One	Dewi Sri	Goddess of Rice	*Kaja-kangin* (Northeast)
Two	Indra	Lord of the Heavens	*Kangin* (East)
Three	Guru	Supreme Teacher	*Kelod-kangin* (Southeast)
Four	Yama	Lord of Hell	*Kelod* (South)
Five	Rudra	Dissolver of Life	*Kelod-kauh* (Southwest)
Six	Brahma	God of Fire	*Kauh* (West)
Seven	Kala	Lord of Darkness	*Kaja-kauh* (Northwest)
Eight	Uma	Mother of all Nature	*Kaja* (North)

ings. The compass rose can be seen in terms of a grid consisting of a rectangle, corresponding to the perimeter wall of the compound, subdivided into nine "squares." Each square represents one of the eight cardinal and intercardinal points of the compass, while the ninth square occupies the center of the rose.

Distance and Position

The first building to be erected in the compound is the householder's sleeping pavilion (*meten*). All subsequent structures are laid out in relation to this starting-out point. The distance between the different buildings in the compound, and their position and proximity to the compound's walls, is critical.

The principal unit of measurement employed is the length of the house owner's foot (*tampak*), and again the number of units for a particular dimension is calculated by reference to the Balinese compass rose. The system works as follows: each of the four cardinal points—and their intermediaries—are associated with a particular deity in the Balinese Hindu pantheon, and as the compound is measured out in paces, the names of the deities are recited (page 8). A single pace is identified with the rice goddess Dewi Sri, two paces with Indra, three paces with Guru, and so on until one arrives at eight paces (Uma), whereupon the cycle begins again.

Layout of the Compound

1 Temporary family shrine
2 *Meten*
3 *Paon*
4 Entrance and *aling-aling* wall

Entrances

Balinese compounds have only one entrance, on the side bordering the street. Entrances define the threshold between inside and out and are viewed ambivalently; although they may admit visitors they may also allow in malign influences. Thus, the entrance belongs to the vile sphere and should therefore be located at the compound's *kelod* end, and to the west. A small wall (*aling-aling*) is often placed directly behind the doorway. This screens off the interior, but more importantly obstructs the entry of malevolent spirits, which are believed to have difficulty making abrupt changes of direction.

There is only one entrance to each Balinese house compound and it is often elaborately decorated with auspicious and powerful symbols, including the god Bhoma, a guardian spirit who wards off evil influences from entering the compound.

Each deity in the Balinese Hindu pantheon is also associated with one of the cardinal directions and a particular set of attributes (see table, page 81) that together determine the number of units employed in setting out the dimensions of individual buildings. The householder's sleeping pavilion, for example, is the most important structure in the compound after the family temple, and for this reason it has to be be located at the *kaja* end of the compound.

Position of the Entrance

The main entrance to the Balinese compound should ideally be placed on the west (*kauh*) side at the seaward (*kelod*) end. For various reasons this is not always possible, in which case the "blind" wall (*aling-aling*) that stands just inside the doorway is designed so that anyone coming into the compound must first proceed toward the *kelod-kauh side* of the compound before they reach the center, around which the main buildings are arranged.

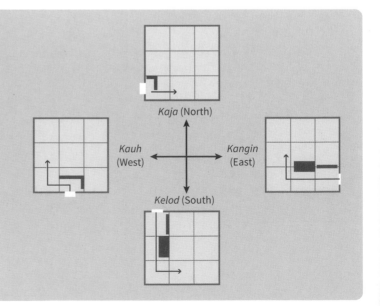

In southern Bali, where most of the island's population live, *kaja* roughly corresponds to north, this being the direction of the central mountain range. Consequently, the sleeping pavilion should be placed eight *tampak*, or multiples thereof, from the *kaja*-most wall, because the number eight is associated with the deity Uma, who in this scheme of things is identified with the north. The cookhouse, or kitchen, on the other hand, should be set out at a distance of six *tampak*, or multiples thereof, to the south of the house owner's pavilion since the number six is identified with Brahma, who is, in turn, associated with fire and with the hearth.

Similar considerations apply for all other structures in the compound. Their relative positions must be carefully worked out in order to ensure that all is for the best in the best of all possible worlds.

The Dwelling Compound

The Balinese residential compound is home to an extended family typically consisting of a married couple, their married sons with their wives and children, their unmarried daughters, and, if they are still alive, the parents of the husband. If a group of brothers decides to stay together, each brother will have his own living quarters within the compound with its own kitchen facilities.

The level inside the compound is generally a little higher than that of the street outside. This serves both a practical and symbolic function. On the one hand, it makes it easier to provide drainage for the compound simply by creating conduits that empty into a ditch running on either side of the road. On the other hand, the superior elevation is part of a hierarchical ordering of space that runs from the street to the family temple

(*sanggah*) situated in the *kaja-kangin* corner of the compound. The family temple is the highest point in the compound, reflecting its status as sacred ground.

The Family Temple

The family temple is set off from the rest of the buildings in the compound by a low wall which provides a sacred enclosure (*pamerajan*) for the family shrines. The relative dimensions of this walled-off space are governed by ritual prescriptions similar to those that regulate the shape and size of the compound as a whole. Different dimensions have different implications. For example, the gods are said to favor a family whose *sanggah* enclosure is only one unit longer than it is wide; even higher esteem is attached to those whose place of worship differs by two units, and great purity where the difference is one of five units. These attributions are not always positive: marriage to an unfaithful wife may be the fate of those where the difference between length and width is eight units. The location of the entrance to the *sanggah* enclosure is also important and should ideally be placed between the sleeping pavilion (*umah meten*) of the family head and the *bale kangin*, the pavilion occupying the eastern side of the central court. A north-facing entrance is considered to be particularly inauspicious.

Gods and Ancestors

The family temple contains a number of different shrines dedicated to both the gods and to family ancestors. The most prominent of the shrines is the *sanggah kamulan*, a small, wooden, house-like construction raised on pillars and standing on a sandstone or brick column. This structure is divided into three compartments, dedicated to the Hindu triumvirate (*trimurti*) of Brahma, Siwa, and Wisnu. Brahma is associated with the male ancestors of the household, while Wisnu is identified with the female ancestors. A Balinese man should build one of these shrines when he marries.

The *sanggah kamulan* stands in the *kaja-kangin* corner of the temple enclosure, together with other ritual structures dedicated to Mother Earth (Ibu Pretiwi) and to the sacred mountains of the island, Gunung Agung and Gunung Batur. The rice goddess, Sri, shares a shrine (*panegtegan*) with the deities of wealth and knowledge, Rambut Sedana and Saraswati, respectively. There may also be an altar dedicated to the sun god, Surya.

Other ritual structures can also be located in the *kaja-kangin* corner of the temple enclosure, dedicated to one or more of several different gods and goddesses. These structures vary according to the status of the head of the family but are often simple,

FAR LEFT **The salients at the four corners of the compound are intended to impede bad feelings arising within the compound from being broadcast abroad and, conversely, to prevent malign influences from entering from outside. These bastions against the passage of malevolency in and out of the compound are called** *paduraksa. Padu* **means "corner" and** *raksa* **means "guardian."**

ABOVE **The** *umah meten* **is the main sleeping pavilion for the head of the household and it occupies pride of place within the compound, in the center of the** *kaja* **or northernmost end.**

thatch-roofed structures. There will also be a number of brick and sandstone columns around the compound where offerings can be placed for the spirits who guard the home and its occupants.

Kangin

Kaja ←

Sleeping, Eating, and Bathing

The Balinese compound appears to lack what Western visitors would recognize as adequate provision for sleeping, eating, and bathing. The head of the family sleeps in the most prestigious pavilion in the compound, the *umah meten*, which he inherits from his parents when they die, situated along the *kaja* wall of the central courtyard. Children and their mothers tend to sleep in the *bale sakepat*, but other family members sleep wherever they choose—typically in one of the open-sided pavilions around the central courtyard (*natar*) or the platform beneath the rice granary. There are seldom any bathing facilities within the compound, though piped water has altered the situation in recent years, and people take their bath in rivers, water conduits and specially constructed bathing pools.

ABOVE **Balinese royal palace compounds are more elaborate versions of the traditional house compound—with larger grounds, grander buildings, gardens and spacious pavilions for guests and ritual performances, but arranged on the same principles. Many palaces are open to visitors and some modern palace replicas like Puri Langon, just north of Ubud (shown here), are designed to be rented out for weddings and private functions.**

Layout of a Typical Residential Compound

1 Entrance.
2 *Aling-aling*, or "blind" wall.
3 *Natar* or *latar*, *sinub westra*, a level, open courtyard in the center of the compound, which is kept free of built structures.
4 *Sanggah*, the family temple.
5 *Umah meten*, a sleeping pavilion for the head of the family.
6 *Bale tiang sanga*, a pavilion for receiving guests.
7 *Bale sakepat*, a pavilion where children and other junior members of the family sleep.

8 *Bale sakenam*, traditionally a place where women do their weaving.
9 and 10 The kitchen (*paon*) and rice barn (*lumbung*), which occupy the "lowest" part of the site, at the seaward (*kelod*) end of the compound. In the *nawa-sanga* system, this is the domain of Wisnu, the preserver and governor. Significantly, Wisnu is identified with female ancestors, the kitchen and granary being primarily regarded as the domain of women.

Twelve-column *umah meten* (main sleeping pavilion)

Bale sakenam (six-column meeting and sleeping pavilion)

House Pavilions

The typical Balinese residential compound consists of a number of different structures grouped around a central courtyard. Each building is associated with a particular function or activity and has a specific location in the family compound. Each structure is classified according to the number of posts used in its construction.

A structure that employs four posts to support the roof is called a *bale sakepat* (*bale* = pavilion, *sakasa* = post, *empat* = four); a *bale sakenam* is a six-post structure (*enam* = six), and so on up to the maximum of twelve posts. Most buildings are raised on a masonry stereobate, or plinth, and are open on one or more sides. The roof is supported by a timber and bamboo frame. Walls, where they exist, are not designed to carry any load, but simply give protection from the elements and provide a degree of privacy.

Umah Meten

The sleeping pavilion (*umah meten*) of the house owner is the first building to be erected after construction of temporary shrines in the *kaja-kangin* corner of the compound. It is located to the west of the family temple at the *kaja* end of the compound. It is a rectangular structure with four solid, windowless walls, and a single entrance in the middle of the elevation facing the center of the compound. The interior consists simply of a

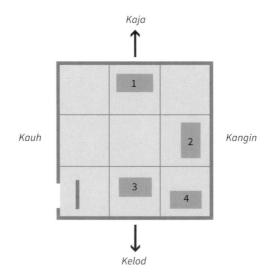

Position of Buildings within a Residential Compound

1 *Umah meten*
2 *Bale sakenam*
3 *Paon*
4 *Lumbung*

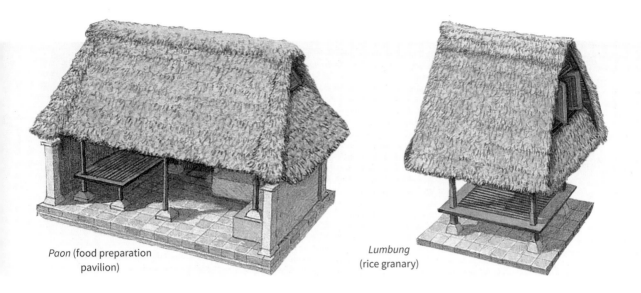

Paon (food preparation pavilion)

Lumbung (rice granary)

BELOW **Contemporary reinterpretations of the classic Balinese pavilion are now widely seen throughout the island—and in other tropical locales—in a myriad of styles, forms and functions.**

pair of wooden sleeping platforms (*pedeman*) positioned on either side of the door.

The *umah meten* of the common man is an eight-pillar structure, but, in the case of higher-caste families, the stereobate is extended to create a veranda or porch in front of the entrance with another line of posts supporting the roof. The *umah meten* is where the family sleeps and keeps its valuables—gold, silver, jewelry, and the family *kris* (ceremonial dagger). It is also traditionally the place for giving birth—the term *meten* is derived from the word *metu*, meaning "to come out" or "to be born."

The building may also be used during periods of ritual restriction, which are required before certain rites of passage that mark significant events in a person's life, such as tooth-filing or the first menstruation. In this respect, the *meten* is perceived in ritual terms as the family womb, a place where children are born and where changes of

status, seen here as a kind of symbolic rebirth, occur. Although normally occupied by the head of the family and his wife, the *umah meten* may be vacated for newlyweds or unmarried girls, for it is the only place in the compound where privacy is available.

LEFT Many Balinese have out-fitted their traditional house compounds with lovely gardens and pergolas and rent rooms or entire pavilions out to tourists as homestays.

BELOW Traditional *lumbung* rice barns have a distinctive curved roof shaped like the hull of an upturned boat. The rice is stored in the upper compartment and a raised platform underneath it serves to prevent rats from climbing up the posts, as well as serving as a sheltered area for sleeping.

Paon

The kitchen is usually a fairly simple structure, built on a low plinth and often employing a gable roof which is easier to construct than the hipped alternative. Earthen charcoal- or wood-burning stoves are built along the rear wall and pots and pans are slung overhead. Traditionally, there would also be large earthenware water storage jars, though a piped water supply is more common today.

Lumbung

The granary is a more elaborate affair than other buildings in the compound. Its floor is raised high off the ground on posts that stand on foundation stones rather than a stereobate or masonry plinth. Sometimes there is an intermediate platform raised a little off the ground, but below the floor of the granary. This provides a cool, shady workplace by day and somewhere to sleep at night. *Lumbung* designs vary from one part of the island to another, but the distinctive hull-shaped roof with horseshoe gable ends can generally be seen in the southern areas. Often one sees wooden discs on top of the foundation posts. These are intended to deter rodents from climbing up and feeding on the rice harvest.

Rice farming is a very special activity in Balinese eyes, rice itself being perceived as a gift of the gods. Not surprisingly, the filling of the granary with a newly harvested crop is an important moment in each agricultural season and it is traditionally accompanied by rituals dedicated to Dewi Sri, who is the goddess of agriculture and fertility. In the past, the newly harvested rice was taken from the fields while still in its panicle and stored directly in the *lumbung*. Nowadays, however, the modern, fast-growing strains of rice are threshed and winnowed in the fields and it is the hulled rice that is taken back to the granary.

Decorative Features

Although the Balinese people are renowned for their artistic and creative energies, Balinese domestic architecture is not subject to a great degree of decorative elaboration or ornamentation, except in the case of royal palaces and the homes of wealthy members of the *triwangsa* castes. Decoration of ordinary houses, where it does occur, is typically reserved for wooden components.

The shafts of house posts may be given a distinctive sculpted profile, while the brackets supporting beams may be enlivened by ornate foliate embellishment. Doors are typically paneled, and carved wooden friezes or ventilation grilles are also commonplace. These decorative elements are painted, but in the case of royal palaces and other important structures, such as the *bale gede* pavilion, may also be gilded with gold leaf.

Masonry walls stand on a stepped foundation, and are topped by a decorative cornice or coping, while the surfaces of the base of pavilions are sometimes ornamented with reliefs. In Majapahit times, in temples and palaces, it was also common to insert ceramics, such as Ming porcelain, into the brickwork.

Location of Decoration

The positioning of decorative features is often significant. Birds, for example, will adorn the upper parts of a structure, being creatures of the air, while representations

ABOVE **Balinese stone carvers are known for their whimsical sense of humor. This carving in Pura Beji Sangsit (in northern Bali) dates from colonial times and shows Dutch musicians serenading a** *naga* **or dragon, the God of the Sea and a symbol of prosperity and protection.**

Doors in Bali, which often incorporate ventilation grilles, are usually paneled and generally surmounted by a decorative frieze. The example here features the leering face of Bhoma, grinning at us rather like the Cheshire cat in Tenniel's illustration for *Alice in Wonderland*.

Beam with a decorative end.

Wooden beams, bamboo rafters, and decorative brackets.

Capital and carved column from a rice barn.

BELOW Painted wooden decoration from a family temple, Sebatu.

of malevolent beings are nearer ground level, reflecting their associations with the infernal nether regions.

In the case of *triwangsa* residences, the family temple in the *kaja-kangin* corner of the compound is surrounded by a perforated wall known as an *ancak saji* wall: a honeycomb effect is created by leaving spaces between the building blocks, after which glazed tiles and other ceramic pieces are inserted in the wall.

One of the most striking images in Balinese iconography is the face of a leering monster, Bhoma, with lolling tongue, bulging eyes, and ferociously large canines. This fearful countenance is typically found over the monumental gateway (*kori agung*) of palaces and temples, in order to drive away malevolent influences.

Palaces and Temples

In royal palaces, much effort and expense goes into the construction of monumental gateways. These resemble temple portals and perform much the same role—to demarcate the realm of ordinary life from some other plane of existence, the one sacred, the other political, though in the traditional scheme of things, the personage of the ruler was as much endowed with a mystical efficacy as with temporal power, for the two were part of the same phenomenon.

On temples, almost every element of the architecture is either carved, painted, or gilded. However, the most important and most elaborate carvings are reserved for the walls and gates, for these form the division between the sacred ground of the temple and the profane ground outside it. During temple festivals, "temporary" ornamentation in the form of bunting, banners, sashes made of brocade or black-and-white checked cloth wrapped around pavilion posts, and woven coconut leaf shade structures add to the overall "decorativeness."

Temple reliefs often depict well-known scenes or episodes from Indian classical literature. The *Ramayana* and the *Mahabharata* epics provide a rich source of inspiration. Other favorites include erotic encounters from the *Arjuna Wiwaha* which portray luscious nymphs making passionate love to the god Arjuna, and charming vignettes from the *tantri* tales, the Balinese equivalent of Aesop's fables from classical Greek literature.

Often there can be a humorous element to these representations. The Mexican painter Miguel Covarrubias, who lived in Bali in the early 1930s, likened the reliefs in north Bali to American-style comic strips. A well-known example at the Pura Dalem, Jagaraga, near Singaraja, shows a car driven by bearded foreigners being held up by a gangster armed with a revolver, while at the nearby Pura Meduwe Karang, in Kubutambahan, there is an image of a European man riding a bicycle which has a lotus flower for a rear wheel. The latter is said to portray the Dutch artist W. O. J. Nieuwen-kamp, who visited Bali in the early years of the 20th century.

Wood and Paint

The Balinese are probably the most prodigious wood carvers in the world and also the most versatile. There are many carving styles, some spawned by the tourism boom, others a result of borrowing from the decorative traditions of other Indonesian islands, yet others stemming from the ability to break free of standard patterns and styles. But nowhere are the Balinese more decorative than in the ornamentation of their architecture, especially the abodes of their gods and the palaces of the nobility.

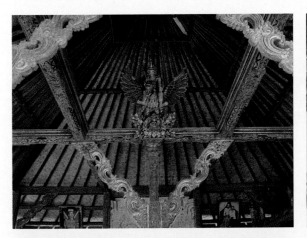

FAR LEFT **Exquisitely carved and colored posts and beams at Puri Anyar, Krambitan.**

LEFT **A highly carved lotus throne (*padmasana*) in Ubud.**

BELOW LEFT **Brightly painted floral carvings topped by a mask on an altar.**

BELOW **Paintings in the traditional *wayang* style on the ceiling of the Kerta Gosa Hall of Justice in the former palace of the kings of Klungkung.**

Balinese Hotels and Resorts

The advent of mass tourism in the past few decades in Bali has had a considerable impact on the physical appearance of Denpasar, the island's capital, and the principal tourist destinations of Sanur, Nusa Dua, Kuta, Seminyak, Canggu, Candi Desa, Lovina and Ubud. With some exceptions, however, there has been a conscious attempt to respect the essential character and to adopt the best aspects of traditional Balinese architecture.

The enormous injection of foreign money into the island's economy, combined with the need to cater for the requirements of these visitors from overseas, has inevitably caused changes to Bali's built environment. Nowhere is this more obvious than in the hotel sector. Driven by the economics of modern tourism, hotel buildings and resorts are reshaping the face of the island.

The Earliest Hotels

The Bali Beach Hotel at Sanur, built in the early 1970s, marked a rather ominous start to the tourist boom. Built in the so-called International Modernist style, its eight stories dominate the skyline of what would other-wise be an idyllic tropical shore, and are out of sympathy with the local surroundings, both architectural and natural. Its white rendered balconies and Y-shaped plan form additional alien elements.

Fortunately, since then there has been a conscious attempt to respect the essential character of Balinese

OPPOSITE Luxury hotel lobbies in Bali often feature traditional elements, like the "Tree of Life" puppets from the *wayang kulit* shadow play on the wall and sculpted lamp holders.

BELOW A four-poster *bale sakepat* serves as a comfortable lounging area in a lush tropical garden by the beach in this five-star Nusa Dua resort

architectural style wherever possible. A "no higher than the palm trees" approach has helped to establish the rules for large-scale hotel development and has inflluenced a generation of hotel buildings which exemplify viable and attractive alternatives to the high-rise Bali Beach Hotel. The notions that a thatched roof makes a building "Balinese" or that tropical resort architecture is nothing more than palm trees and swimming pools have also been dispelled by the conscious attempt to create buildings which are not only functional but which celebrate what Bali has to offer in terms of traditional building concepts (such as an ingrained sense of spatial order), traditional construction techniques, and the inclusion of Balinese materials and crafts.

LEFT **The new "Bali Style" resort design vocabulary developed in the 1980s has now spread around the world and is seen in holiday resorts in Hawaii, the Carribean and the Mediterranean.**

BELOW **Balinese** *lumbung* **or rice barns have been enlarged and repurposed into two-story luxury villas in a resort hotel.**

The focal point of the Amankila resort, perched on cliffs above the ocean on Bali's east coast, is the dramatic three terraced swimming pools whose edges appear to dissolve into the ocean.

Many international hotels have successfully modeled their chalet-style accommodation on Balinese pavilions, albeit with the addition of modern facilities such as running water and air conditioning, while other regional forms have also been adopted and adapted to extend the range of building types. The layout and landscaping of the Bali Hilton at Nusa Dua, for example, recalls the Javanese palace, or *kraton*, while the Indies-style architecture of the colonial era provides a historical precedent for an imaginative synthesis of Indonesian and European architectural traditions.

Incorporation of Local Forms

As we have seen in this book, in Balinese culture, the universe has a tripartite cosmologcal model which can be mapped on to the topography of the island of Bali. Similarly, architecture follows this tripartite division, reflected in the base, the walls, and the roof. These three essentials—a heavy base, a lightweight structure of posts, and a hovering roof—maintain the harmony of man, architecture, and landscape. Hotel architects, primarily foreigners, were quick to see that the various forms and types of traditional Balinese buildings responded adequately and appropriately to both the climate and to local cultural beliefs. In particular, they were quick to incorporate the *bale*, the rectangular, open-sided pavilion with its steeply pitched thatched roof.

The appropriation and the manipulation of local forms for new applications does run the risk of trivializing or otherwise corrupting traditional architectural values—the inappropriate use of temple structures is a case in point. At the same time, the incorporation of local elements as adornment for structures that would otherwise be entirely utilitarian or functional encourages the tendency towards pastiche, which similarly devalues local architectural traditions. Both these tendencies are evident in Bali.

Landscape as a Design Element

One of the most powerful and seductive components of the Bali Hotel experience is the landscaping. The 390-room Bali Hyatt, opened in 1973, and the complete antithesis of the nearby Hotel Bali Beach, set new standards in Bali in garden design. Although Balinese houses do not have gardens, but rather an open compound, lush, tropical gardens became the hallmark of the Hyatt and subsequent hotels. Largely the brainchild of Made Wijaya (the Australian Michael White), whose style of landscaping has been described as "loud and lush with piquant accents Balinese," the Bali Hyatt gardens influenced other hotel architects and landscape designers to adopt garden strategies and to look to the natural landscape as a design element.

Inspired Designs

In Bali today, there are a great many instances of truly inspired hotel and resort designs that incorporate the best of traditional Balinese architecture, combined with carefully structured landscapes. These highly sophisticated "architectures of welcome" provide visitors with

the feeling that Bali is truly an island of the gods, a refuge between the mountains and the sea.

Three Aman resort properties of the visionary developer Adrian Zecha led the way in the 1990s. At the Amandari ("peaceful spirits"), northwest of Ubud, the main buildings represent the various types (and scales) of Balinese *bale*, while the public facilities are concentrated around the swimming pool, which is shaped as a terraced rice field, its edge disappearing into nothing. Each of the hotel's detached villas, thatched with *alang-alang*, lies behind high *paras* walls, like a traditional Balinese house compound. The Amanusa ("peaceful island") is located on two knolls above Bali's southernmost peninsula, the valley between dammed to form a huge swimming pool. The Amankila ("peaceful hill") resort in Karangasem, with its three terraced swimming pools, each with dramatic "infinity" edges, and its colonnades, is modeled on the nearby water palace at Taman Ujung, the complex of pools and pavilions built by the last ruler of Karangasem.

Appealing to the senses, the Ibah resort in Ubud consists of a series of thatched villas strung along the

banks of the Campuan River amid a densely planted landscape. On a larger scale, the Four Seasons Resort at Jimaran Bay extends the concept of the hotel as village. The hotel's 147 villas, organized into a series of villages, tumble down a sloping site accompanied by effusive landscaping.

Taking its inspiration from the Bali Aga village at Tenganan, and in particular the form of the *bale agung*, or great hall, the Balina Serai near Candiasa in east Bali exemplifies the restrained, somewhat austere "block" design of Bali Aga architecture with its use of massive bases capped by thatched roofs. The stone flags set within the lawns in front of the lobby also echo the paving techniques at Tenganan.

Total exclusivity and total immersion in the Bali experience are offered by the individualized architectural attention paid at the Begawan Giri estate at Ubud. The estate comprises five residences and 22 suites, each designed after a specific region or traditional building type.

The Four Seasons at Sayan offers a completely new image of the Bali hotel. A striking piece of aerial

sculpture, it has been variously described as an elliptical lotus pond held aloft by a giant earth sculpture; an offering to the gods of fruit, rice and delicacies, piled high and carried on the head to the temple; a dish of lotus flowers; a shallow dish held aloft by an outstretched arm where water is sprinkled on a new guest as a sign of welcome. Like the hotels above, it is a highly seductive "architecture of welcome."

ABOVE FAR LEFT **The main pavilion of "Forest in the Mist," one of the five palatial residences in the Como Begawan Giri estate. Aged teak planks and iron-wood shingles are used extensively for flooring and roofing.**

ABOVE MIDDLE **The boundary between indoors and outdoors is removed in many modern Balinese villas with the use of sliding glass doors that can be opened during the day and closed at night.**

ABOVE RIGHT **The Four Seasons Resort Bali at Sayan, situated in an unspoiled tropical valley setting, provides a completely new image for a Balinese resort hotel. The focus of this resort is a massive three-story cylinder set on a valley floor, which opens out on to a large, elliptical lotus pond. Large spaces framed by natural ivory stone columns (below) allow panoramic views of the surrounding jungle and rice fields.**

Contemporary Balinese Villas

Bali has long exerted the power to seduce and stir the romantic imagination, and over the last 100 years many people have set up home there. Although most newcomers, enchanted by traditional Balinese architectural forms, have chosen to build their homes in vernacular "Bali style," eclectic forms and new materials have led in more recent years to the development of a "new tropical internationalism."

The first half of the 20th century saw the emergence of Sanur, on the eastern tip of Bali's southern coast, as prime real estate for those enthralled by Bali. Among the luminaries who built beach bungalows were Jack Mershon and his choreographer wife Katharane who, with Walter Spies, invented the *kecak* "monkey" dance; writer Vicki Baum (*A Tale from Bali*); anthropologists Jane Belo (*Trance in Bali*) and Margaret Mead, and art dealer brothers Hans and Rolf Neuhaus. Bali's most famous expatriate of this era was, however, the German artist-writer-musician Walter Spies, who had arrived to settle in Bali in 1927, and had built for himself a beautiful house and studio in the Balinese style at the confluence of two rivers at Campuan, west Ubud. Decorated with local paintings and carvings, it was the precursor of many similar houses built by Westerners who followed in his footsteps. Spies and these early "Baliphiles" hosted a steady stream of celebrity visitors to the island in the 1930s, including Charlie Chaplin, Barbara Hutton, Doris Duke, and Harold Nicholson. In particular, Spies' house—and his hospitality—became "the doorway to Bali" for many travelers.

Not long after Indonesia proclaimed independence in 1945, Sanur witnessed the beginnings of an expatriate building boom led by the Belgian painter Adrien Le Mayeur, whose former studio-home on the beach north of the Grand Bali Beach Hotel is now a museum. Australian artists Ian Fairweather and Donald Friend also chose picturesque Sanur for their beach retreats. Friend lived in imperial splendor with an in-house gamelan, a huge garden of exotic plants, and a superb collection of art within the grounds of the Batu Jimbar estate. Since then, thousands of foreigners, many of whom are engaged in some kind of artistic pursuit, have made Bali their home.

The Development of "Bali Style" Residences
Western tourism to Bali reached an unprecedented level in the late 1960s and early 1970s. Among the arrivals were those interested in the spiritual and aesthetic aspects of Balinese culture, who found refuge in the island's mysticism, as opposed to those who came

The German artist-writer-musician Walter Spies was one of the first among a cosmopolitan group of art-loving expatriates to settle in Bali in the late 1920s. His simple thatched house, set in lush gardens overlooking the picturesque River Oos, a kilometer northwest of Ubud, has been renovated but still stands as part of a bungalow complex forming the Hotel Campuan. Spies set a precedent for vernacular-style houses built by foreign residents in Bali.

Elements of the New "Bali Style"

Open-air walkways, spacious verandas and wooden decks, thatched pavilions in garden settings, courtyards containing pools and temple carvings, living rooms that invite the outside landscaping in, and open-to-the-sky bathrooms are all distinctive features of what has become known worldwide as "Bali style"—a style that has been copied prodigiously throughout the tropical world.

CLOCKWISE FROM TOP LEFT **A covered walkway, flanked by lotus ponds, links different parts of this home. A thatched *bale* and deck next to a swimming pool are given privacy by a carved sandstone lattice wall. Built on a platform atop a lily pond, this *bale* is serviced by air cooled from the water. An old tree, emerging from a bed of white pebbles, shadows this open-to-the sky bathroom.**

ABOVE **Large *alang-alang*** thatched roofs, with their softer contours, are increasingly being replaced with ironwood shingled roofs with strong, geometric compositions that require less maintenance.

LEFT **The open bathroom has** become a signature feature of Balinese-style resorts, often with gardens and open-air bathing areas.

merely for the sun and sea. Many stayed on to establish cottage industries. Others built small, basic houses and inns (*losmen*) in the tourist areas. More sophisticated dwellings, supervised by Western architects, also began to appear in Sanur at this time, considered the most trendy part of the island.

It was the extraordinary expansion of mass tourism in the 1980s and 1990s, however, which was to have the greatest impact on Bali's built environment. Hundreds of hotels and luxury resort complexes replaced the modest *losmen* as tourist accommodation. These were the years of the Oberoi Hotel and the Bali Hyatt, the first responses to the problem of how tropical architecture could and should be adapted for the tourist industry in Bali.

A new wave of people coming to Bali for commercial reasons, mainly in the import-export sector, also began to build their own private homes, choosing pavilion or palace or mansion styles, mimicking the traditional Balinese compound, and taking traditional architectural elements, but attempting to import Western standards— not always successfully.

A new, more sophisticated, affluent, and discriminating breed of visitor in the mid-1990s led a demand for improved building standards and to major changes

TOP **A morning yoga session in an open pavilion followed by breakfast overlooking an infinity-edge pool with palm trees and rice terraces in the background are all part of today's unique "Bali experience."**

ABOVE **Open-air baths and showers were pioneered in Balinese resorts in the 1970s and are now commonplace worldwide.**

in the development and quality of public buildings, especially hotels. Not only better service but higher levels of accommodation and more aesthetic appeal guaranteed high occupancy rates. Interiors have undergone a transformation, too. Artistic collaboration between outsiders and the Balinese has resulted in the ubiquitous stone carvings and wooden sculptures of early interiors being replaced by Bali-inspired, international-standard decor accessories.

In the private sector, long-term residents wanted less makeshift places to live. In their desire to settle in Bali and forge a new life, they sought to replicate the comforts of home but to reintepret these in a "Balinese" way. They built—or had built for them—tropical homes that took elements from their own heritages and combined these with Balinese influences and styles. The result was a plethora of residences in many different designs, but all loosely gathered under the umbrella term of "Bali style." To accompany the architecture came the interior design: a type of outdoor-indoor living style that has its roots in the climate of the tropics, but its applications in Western traditions of comfortable furniture and furnishings.

New Tropical Internationalism

Recent trends in residential architecture suggest that the world-renowned and increasingly popular "Bali style" is now evolving into an eclectic, international style, propelled by architectural and design trends from outside rather than from within Bali. Feeding off the innate creativity of the Balinese, and bringing new ideas and technologies from outside, foreign architects and designers are reworking and reinterpreting the much-touted concept of "Bali style." All over the island, startlingly original homes are the result of exciting collaborations between Balinese building techniques and contemporary vision. Tradition is being challenged by modernity, organic materials are vying with metal and plastic, and high-tech components are dualing with hand-crafted accessories.

Significantly, Balinese pavilion-style architecture is being replaced with a more contemporary vision of space; if the *bale* persists, it is more likely to be constructed of marble or stone than wood and thatch.

Strong lines and geometric forms now sometimes replace the softer *alang-alang* roofs. Extensive and imaginative use of stone, glass, and ceramics complements Balinese shingles, wood, *alang-alang* thatch, and bamboo. More is being made of the textures of structural elements, as well as the style of interior decoration. The ability and flexibity of local craftsmen who can copy-and-craft simultaneously, and the island's abundance of natural materials, have led to the development of stylish, cutting-edge home decor items. A new cosmopolitanism, the result of tapping into trends from outside rather than from within Bali, is flourishing in this island of the gods.

This cosmopolitanism has had global repercussions. Throughout the tropical world, from Bombay to the Bahamas, from Thailand to the Philippines, the originality of expression, rising quality, and intense creativity of Bali's private residences and of its organic-based decor collections have become the new benchmark for tropical living and tropical design.

ABOVE LEFT **An open-concept living room pavilion in a private villa. As in traditional Balinese houses, the bedroom and kitchen/dining room pavilions are often separate structures.**

LEFT **Local materials are combined with an international design style in this house. The change of flooring defines the outdoor-indoor transition.**

RIGHT **Natural materials are used not only to face walls and floors but to create new artefacts, panels, and pieces of furniture.**

NEXT SPREAD **A modern interpretation of the traditional *balé*, a shady, open-sided area for relaxation, as shown by this photo. The horizontal structure of the terrace above is an interesting contrast to the slope of the shingled roofs—the terrace is a good place to appreciate the beautiful landscaping.**

Gardens and Water Features

The close integration of landscape and architecture is a concept well suited to the tropics and nowhere is this more visible than in Bali. The island is extraordinarily blessed by Nature. Its traditional temples and palaces have also influenced the compositions of gardens. In more contemporary times, resort hotels have emerged as leaders in the exploration of innovative ways to merge nature with the work of man.

Traditional Gardens in Bali

In contrast to the overcrowded abundance of Bali's natural landscape (*ramé*), traditional gardens in Bali are characterized by empty stillness (*sepi*). The Balinese house compound has no garden in the Western sense of the word. It is a bare and simple working space of free-standing pavilions, the family temple, and a neatly swept ground of packed earth with perhaps one or two isolated trees such as frangipani behind the *aling-aling* screen wall. Often the trees are planted to one side of the compound, sometimes in pots, and there may be one or two other potted flowering plants added for decoration.

Nor are gardens an integral part of most Balinese temples. Instead, mighty banyan trees, called *waringan*

in Balinese, form landmarks in front of temples—as well as at major crossroads and in the forecourts of palaces. Their multiple trunks and aerial roots, hanging down like thick hair, are a stupendous sight. The roots not only play host to a range of ferns and other plants but are a favorite haunt of invisible spirits.

Royal gardens and garden temples consist of pavilions with ponds in or around them, often filled with lotuses, and a few trees. Fountains and water spouts carved in the form of *naga* snakes, elephants, or demonic creatures are a common feature of the water works. These gardens are thus a combination of art and nature but they also demonstrate the concept of *sepi*.

Modern Gardens in Bali

In recent years, the *ramé* end of the spectrum has come more prominent. Government policies have encouraged the Balinese to diversify their diets and grow a wider range of plants in their compounds as well as to beautify them with flower beds. Locally owned hotels and restaurants have incorporated trees and vines and lotus ponds on their premises. But it was the arrival of foreign residents to the island, and later the tourist boom, which was to have the greatest impact on gardens in Bali. The hilly countryside, steep ravines, and meandering streams around Ubud offered foreign residents the opportunity for dramatic, multi-level plantings. Others

LEFT **The Matahari Garden at the Bali Hyatt features stepped terraces leading down to a lotus pond. The 14-hectare Bali Hyatt garden is not only the largest hotel garden by far in Bali—it occupies 75 percent of the total hotel area—but is also the most beautiful and influential. its impressive design concepts, utilizing huge planter boxes, jungle-like courtyards, water gardens, themed plantings, terraces, pathways, and specially commissioned statuary, have inspired a host of others gardens within and outside Bali.**

sought to merge their gardens with the surrounding landscape, especially Bali's rice terraces. Yet others emulated the rather formal patterns of royal gardens, making use of water, courtyards, pavilions, statuary and a limited number of harmoniously placed trees and plants.

Resort Hotel Landscaping

The success of many hotels and resorts in Bali is not due just to the careful design and dramatic scale of their buildings but also to their gardens. A crucial figure behind the new landscape movement was Australian Michael White who had arrived in Bali in 1973 but by 1975 had assumed the Balinese name of Made Wijaya. His first garden, in 1978, was for house "C" in the Batu Jimbar estate designed by the famous Sri Lankan architect Geoffrey Bawa. His style of landscaping, which exploits the exuberant potential of local tropical plants and combines these with English traditions of textural contrasts and bright accents, was soon to be found in several hotels in the archipelago including, in Bali, the Bali Hyatt, Amandari, and the Four Seasons Resort at Jimbaran Bay, as well as in numerous private gardens in Bali for both permanent and part-time residents.

TOP **Contemporary hotel pools and gardens in Bali today provide a sense of luxurious intimacy, with details that echo the royal water gardens of East Bali (see pages 40–43).**

ABOVE **Interconnecting plant-filled ponds, and statuary, such as these at Villa Bebek, Made Wijaya's studio-home in Sanur, are synonymous today with "Bali style."**

Wijaya's work at the Bali Hyatt, in particular, established the importance of landscape as an important component of the Bali hotel experience. The Bali Hyatt landscape offers not only a comprehensive collection of ornamental plants gathered from many parts of the tropical world, but also a beguiling variety of landscaping features, including terraces, courtyards, and water gardens. Added to these are Balinese-style structures, such as *kukul* towers and split *candi bentar* gateways, and the lanterns, decorative terra-cotta fountains, reliefs, stone jars, and the fierce-faced guardian figures and other statuary which have become synonymous worldwide with Bali and "Bali style." Because of the success of the Bali Hyatt gardens, many Bali hotels now combine carefully structured landscapes of lotus ponds and floating pavilions at the lobby, restaurant and bar areas. Beyond these public areas, the residential components of the hotel luxuriate in a romantic profusion of hibiscus, bougainvillea, frangipani, orchids, and palms.

TOP LEFT **Villas with plunge pools built into steep hillsides near Ubud often have views of lush palm trees and rice terrraces that echo the villa at Campuan designed by the painter Walter Spies in the 1930s, and have now become an international design template.**

LEFT **This modernist landscape in a secluded valley in Ubud is a contrast to the usual jungle-like profusion. The lawn complements the variety of palms, ground cover, and decorative plantings.**

ABOVE **Sheer edges and dark stone paving add to the minimalist composition of this rectangular infinity pool at the Alila Ubud.**

109

Water Features

Water is not only the source of life for the Balinese but is also a wonderful cooling element in the hot, humid climate. It is no surprise, therefore, that nearly every architect and landscape artist connected with Bali incorporates some kind of water feature in their designs. These range from cool ponds filled with blooming lotuses and water lilies to cascades, fountains and springs, and from open-to-the-sky bathrooms to atmospheric swimming pools.

Water is a unifying theme in modern courtyard gardens, which often comprise a central swimming pool surrounded by various interconnecting ponds filled with lotuses and other water plants. Mossy statues, fountains, and stepping stones both entertain and add to the overall exotic ambience. At Villa Bebek, Made Wijaya's studio-home in Sanur, a lap pool forms the centerpiece of the compound. Around the pool are ten buildings, each connected by a network of paths, pergolas, gates, terraces, and garden walls, and some 50 small courts. Ponds act as barriers between the buildings and help to cool the surroundings.

Natural springs are not only an essential landscape feature in much of Bali but an integral architectural element, feeding rock pools, swimming pools, and other water features. At the Begawan Giri estate, several rock pools, framed by timber decks and lush vegetation, have been created by capturing a 20-meter natural spring waterfall. Many open-to-the-air bathrooms on the estate utilize the natural spring. Minimalistic outdoor showers, made of bamboo pipes on stone bases, are also fed by the same spring.

The use of overflow, or infinity-edge, pools and the horizon—whether in a tropical valley setting as at the Alila, or beside a beach as at the Legian—is given full reign in Bali. Complementing these, and adding to the seductive Bali experience, are jacuzzi plunge pools set in private vegetation-shrouded nooks.

ABOVE LEFT Water features like this lap pool are central elements in the new Bali resort style along with open living spaces modelled on the *bale* of traditional Balinese houses.

LEFT The open-air bathroom at the "Tirta Ening" villa in the Como Begawan Giri estate near Ubud includes a huge bathtub carved from a 6-tonne piece of solid rock.

Glossary

adat tribal law; tradition; customs

adegan height of the posts of a building, determined by measurements taken from a house owner's body

alang-alang grass thatch (*Imperata* sp.) used as roofing material

aling-aling "blind," or free-standing, wall behind the gateway to the innermost courtyard of a temple complex

alun-alun Javanese term for a village square

a musti unit of measurement, the width of a closed hand with the thumb on top

ancak saji tracery wall enclosing a palace courtyard

apit lawang paired shrines flanking gateways leading into courtyards, where offerings are placed for the guardians of a temple

bacingah village square

bale pavilion

bale agung local assembly hall

bale banjar community meeting hall

bale gede open-sided pavilion on twelve posts, with a pointed roof

bale gong pavilion for gamelan performances

bale kambang water pavilion

bale kukul drum tower

bale sakepat pavilion where children and other junior members of a family sleep

bancingah village square

banjar neighborhood or ward

bedugul roofless shrine, often found in rice fields

bhuwah world of human beings

Brahma the creator; one of the Hindu trinity

brahmana priest caste

buhr the underworld

candi Javanese temple with stepped, pyramidal roof

candi bentar ceremonial split gateway

depa unit of measurement, from fingertip to fingertip when the arms are held out horizontally

desa village

desa adat customary laws

dewa/dewi god/goddess

Dewi Sri goddess of rice and prosperity

Durga Siwa's wife in an evil manifestation

hasta unit of measurement, from the elbow to the fingertip

ijuk black thatch from the sugar palm (*Arenga pinnata* sp.) used for roofing

jaba outermost of three temple courtyards

jaba tengah middle courtyard

jeroan innermost of three temple courtyards

kahyangan tiga collective term for the three temples in a village

kaja upstream, toward the mountain

kangin east

kauh west

kelod downhill, toward the sea

kori agung monumental gateway of palaces and temples

kuren separate households in Bali Aga villages

lontar "book" of palm leaves cut into strips and bound together by a string; engraved with an iron stylus then blackened with soot

lumbung rice granary

Mahabharata Hindu epic; centers on the story of the dynastic struggles between five Pandawa brothers and their cousins, the Korawa

Majapahit Hindu-Buddhist kingdom of 13th-14th century east Java; great influence on Balinese culture

meru wooden house-like shrine with a masonry base and multitiered roof

meten sleeping pavilion

naga serpent

nawa-sanga Balinese compass rose

ngaben cremation

odalan festival

padmasana eight-leafed "lotus seat" shrine, the resting place for the gods in a temple; the eight leaves are for eight gods of eight directions

pamerajan sacred enclosure for family shrines

paon cookhouse, kitchen

paras volcanic ash sandstone used for walls and for carvings on temples

pedanda priest

pedeman sleeping platform

pekarangan walled compound, enclosure

pemangku lay priest at a temple

pesantian pavilion for performing ritual invocations

pratima small wooden effigy

pura temple

pura dalem temple of the dead

pura desa main village temple

pura panataran royal temple

pura puseh ancestral temple

puri palace

rahi unit of measurement for house posts, the length between the base of the thumb and the tip of the index finger

sad kahyangan the six great sanctuaries in Bali

sanggah household or family temple

saka Hindu Balinese lunar calendar

satriya princely caste of royalty and warriors

sawah irrigated rice field

Siwa the destroyer; one of the Hindu trinity

subak local rice cooperative

sudra commoner caste

swah the heavens

tajen cockfighting

tampak principal unit of measurement, the length of the house owner's foot

tirtha holy water

trimurti Hindu triumvirate of Brahma, Siwa, and Wisnu

triwangsa three noble castes consisting of royalty and warriors, priests, and merchants

tumpang tiered, pyramidal-shaped roof

umah meten sleeping pavilion of the house owner

umpak stone column base of a building

Wisnu the preserver; one of the Hindu trinity

wantilan cockfighting pavilion

weisa merchant caste

wuku sacred Balinese calendar

"Books to Span the East and West"

Tuttle Publishing was founded in 1832 in the small New England town of Rutland, Vermont [USA]. Our core values remain as strong today as they were then—to publish best-in-class books which bring people together one page at a time. In 1948, we established a publishing outpost in Japan—and Tuttle is now a leader in publishing English-language books about the arts, languages and cultures of Asia. The world has become a much smaller place today and Asia's economic and cultural influence has grown. Yet the need for meaningful dialogue and information about this diverse region has never been greater. Over the past seven decades, Tuttle has published thousands of books on subjects ranging from martial arts and paper crafts to language learning and literature—and our talented authors, illustrators, designers and photographers have won many prestigious awards. We welcome you to explore the wealth of information available on Asia at www.tuttlepublishing.com.

Published by Tuttle Publishing, an imprint of Periplus Editions (HK) Ltd.

www.tuttlepublishing.com

Copyright © 2023 Periplus Editions (HK) Ltd

ISBN: 978-0-8048-5275-3

26 25 24 23   10 9 8 7 6 5 4 3 2 1

Printed in China   2304EP

TUTTLE PUBLISHING® is a registered trademark of Tuttle Publishing, a division of Periplus Editions (HK) Ltd.

Distributed by:

North America, Latin America and Europe
Tuttle Publishing
364 Innovation Drive, North Clarendon, VT 05759-9436 U.S.A.
Tel: (802) 773 8930; Fax: (802) 773 6993
info@tuttlepublishing.com; www.tuttlepublishing.com

Indonesia
PT Java Books Indonesia, Kawasan Industri Pulogadung,
JI. Rawa Gelam IV No. 9, Jakarta 13930
Tel: (62) 21 4682-1088; Fax: (62) 21 461-0206
crm@periplus.co.id; www.periplus.com

Asia Pacific
Berkeley Books Pte Ltd
3 Kallang Sector #04-01,Singapore 349278.
Tel: (65) 6741-2178; Fax: (65) 6741-2179
inquiries@periplus.com.sg; www.tuttlepublishing.com

Photo Credits

(T = top; B = below; R = right; L = left)

Luca Invernizzzi Tettoni: backcover: bottom row R, p4 top row L, p15B, L, p31B, p40B, p67T, p91B (4 photos), p95, p96L, p97R, p98, p99 top row L & R, 2nd row R, p102B, R, p106, p107B, p108B, p109, p110B

Dreamstime: p31 middle (© Fauzirizal); p74B (© Artem Beliaikin); p75T (© Christophe Amerijckx); p75B (© Edmund Lowe); p8T, L (© Oleg Breslavtsev); backcover: 2nd row L, p35T (© Tuayai)

Istockphoto: p33T (© scottiebumich); backcover: 2nd row R, p42 T (© miralex); p43 (© Terry/Lawrence)

Shutterstock: backcover: top row ext L, p5 top row R, p16T, L, p92 (© 365_visuals); p2 (© R7 Photo); p4 top row R, p23B (© Aleksandar Todorovic); p5B, R, p59B (© Anges van der Logt); p20 middle L (© Artem Beliaikin); pp8/9T (© Artem Gorlanov); p88T (© AstroStar); backcover: bottom row middle, p76 (© Audrey_S); p69T (© ben bryant); p39L (© BGStock72); p61L (© Boyloso); cover's front flap, p101T (© Bucha Natallia); p25T (© Cezary Wojtkowski); p4 bottom row R, p55B, R, p63R (CHEN WS); p46T (© Chokiniti-Studio); p51 B (© Claudine Van Massenhove); p66B (© Constance Stanchu); backcover: bottom row L, p45 (© crbellette); backcover: top row R, p78T (© De Visu); p88B (© Diaz Radityo); p102T (© diyben); p35B (©

Dudarev Mikhail); p66T (© Efried); p21L (© Eky Studio); back ends, p32, pp36/37, p56R (© Elizaveta Galitckaia); p53 (© Em Campos); p73T (© ESstock); p42B (© Fotos593); p15T (© Gabor Kovacs Photography); p37R (© Galina Savina); p101B (© GaudiLab); p47T, p16T, R, p24B, p28, p89 (© Gekko Gallery); cover: main photo & spine (© Guitar photographer); p59T (© guruXOX); p94B (© Happy Auer); p13R (© Hendranyoman); p33B, p34 middle (© imageBROKER.com); p20T, R (© Imagentle); p83L (© Ingrid Pakats); p94T (© jaja); p20B, L (© JHMimaging); pp96/97 middle (© JR-stock); p17L & R, pp54/55 middle (© Julius Bramanto); p49 (© kravka); p5T, L (© Kristian Forkel); pp60/61T (© Liem Men Sang); p93 (© Maciej Czekjewski); p8B, L (© magicinfoto); p62B (© MangPor Photolista); p74T (© Maria Kazakova1); p84 (© mariashkin); p25B, p62T (© MARIO AND SUPRIA); p31T, R (© Marius Dobilas); p5B, L, p77R (© Meniga.id); pp68/69 (© Mistroshenkov Ilia); p27T (© Muslianshah Masrie); p16R, T&B (© Nadezda Murmakova); p63 middle (© nicolasdecorte); p82L (© Odd Hackwelder); p11R, p13L, p73B, p108T, p110T (© OlegD); p50 (© Pav-Pro Photography Ltd); p64, p67B, T (© Phraisohn Siripool); p38 (© Piotr Piatrouski); p10L (© project1photography); p54L (© Puspa Mawarni168); pp70/71 (© R.M. Nunes); p72 (© raditya); p83R (© raga Jenyana); backcover: top row middle, p11L (© ranguin remi); p2 (© R7 Photo); p107T (© RF97); p87 (© Robert Haandrikman); p20T, L (© sakkarin sapu); p34B (© Sony Herdiana); p65 (© Supathin Khayanrai); front ends (© Tavarius); p23T, p85 (© Tebha Workspace); p63T (© Thien Eu); p71T (© Tony Calandruccio); p7B, R (© tooman); pp40/41 T (© tr3gin); p34T (© Travel-Fr); p10R (© Vineet Achari); p47B, R (© Visan Khankasem); p100B, (© Visionsi); p21T, R, p79B (© Vladislav T. Jirousek); p51T (© Zuzha)